"The Lizard, aside from his feet,

    So much like a serpent appears,

    That a glance at him near where we sit

    Scarce fails to awaken our fears."

—*The Rev. Jonathan Fisher,* Scripture Animals, *1845*

Lizards

*A Natural History of Some Uncommon
Creatures—Extraordinary Chameleons,
Iguanas, Geckos, and More*

Text by David Badger
Photography by John Netherton

Voyageur Press

Dedication

For John
November 16, 1948 – March 15, 2001

Acknowledgments

The author and photographer wish to express their gratitude to the following for their assistance with this book: Nicole Atteberry; Richard Campbell, director, School of Journalism, Middle Tennessee State University; Mike Carlton; Jim and Jamie R. Clark; Eastman Kodak; Mary Fleming; Travis Foust; Lynn and Roland Frasier; Shelly Graham; Christopher R. Harris; Glenn Himebaugh; David Kledzik, assistant curator of reptiles, St. Augustine Alligator Farm; Greg Lepera, curator of herpetology, Jacksonville Zoological Gardens; Fred Marcum; Dale McGinnity, curator of ectotherms, Nashville Zoo; Joyce Miller; Nikon Inc.; Rachel Petrie; Chris Richards and the staff of The Aquatic Critter, Nashville; Jim Vines; and Joe Wasilewski.

We would also like to thank Michael Dregni, editorial director of Voyageur Press, for his faith in this project and keeping it alive and on track; and the author appreciates the literary vigilance and outstanding editorial contributions to the manuscript made by Kari Cornell.

We are particularly indebted to Brian Miller, professor of biology at Middle Tennessee State University, for reviewing the entire manuscript and offering invaluable suggestions throughout all stages of the book. We also gratefully acknowledge Victoria Jackson for her dedication and assistance with John's photographic collection.

Special thanks are also extended to the author's wife, Sherry, and son, Jeff, and to the photographer's three sons, Josh, Jason, and Erich Netherton, for their unfailing support and good humor during the entire saurian undertaking.

Edited by Kari Cornell
Designed by Maria Friedrich
Printed in China

03   04   05   06   07   5   4   3   2   1

Library of Congress Cataloging-in-Publication Data
Badger, David P.
  Lizards : a natural history of some uncommon creatures, extraordinary chameleons, iguanas, geckos, and more / text by David Badger ; photography by John Netherton.
      p. cm.
    Includes bibliographical references (p. 154–155).
    ISBN 0-89658-520-4
    1. Lizards.   I. Netherton, John. II. Title.
  QL666.L2B14 2003
  597.95—dc21

2002012138

Distributed in Canada by Raincoast Books
9050 Shaughnessy Street
Vancouver, B.C. V6P 6E5

Published by Voyageur Press, Inc.
123 North Second Street
P.O. Box 338
Stillwater, MN 55082 U.S.A.
651-430-2210, fax 651-430-2211
books@voyageurpress.com
www.voyageurpress.com

Educators, fundraisers, premium and gift buyers, publicists, and marketing managers: Looking for creative products and new sales ideas? Voyageur Press books are available at special discounts when purchased in quantities, and special editions can be created to your specifications. For details, contact the marketing department at 800-888-9653.

On the cover and frontispiece:
Madagascan giant day gecko

On the title pages:
Lizard tracks, discovered by a Navajo guide shortly after sunrise, are visible in the sand dunes of Monument Valley in northeastern Arizona. The photographer lay on his stomach and used a 15mm lens to enhance the spatial relationship between the tracks and the horizon.

On the title pages, small photo:
Namib Desert gecko

Facing the dedication page:
Crested gecko

Facing page:
Panther chameleon

Table of Contents

Jackson's chameleon

Introduction   11

Chapter 1
Lizards and Humans   19

Chapter 2
Physical Characteristics and Behavior   31

Shape and Size   31
Skin and Coloration   36
Limbs and Locomotion   42
Eyes and Vision   47
Ears and Hearing   52
Smell and Taste   55
Teeth and Venom   57
Tails and Autotomy   61
Internal Anatomy   65
Thermoregulation   68
Reproduction   71
Communication   74
Defense Strategies   78
Predation   84
Hibernation   86

Chapter 3
Families and Species   89

Jackson's Chameleon   90
Panther Chameleon   92
Flap-Necked Chameleon   95
Mountain Chameleon   96
Green Anole   98
Jamaican Giant Anole   100
Madagascan Giant Day Gecko   102
Crested Gecko   105

Leopard Gecko   106
Fat-Tailed Gecko   109
Namib Desert Gecko   111
Five-Lined Skink   112
Prehensile-Tailed Skink   114
Gila Monster   116
Eastern Glass Lizard   118
Short-Horned Lizard   120
Collared Lizard   123
Six-Lined Racerunner   123
Fence Lizard   124
Granite Spiny Lizard   126
Lava Lizards   127
Green Iguana   129
Marine Iguana   130
Galápagos Land Iguanas   132
Rhinoceros Iguana   134
Black Tree Monitor   137
Gould's Monitor   137
Crocodile Monitor   140
Komodo Dragon   142

Chapter 4
Lizard Conservation   147

Bibliography   154

Index   157

About the Author and Photographer
   160

Introduction

L izards are simply spectacularly beautiful terrestrial fish," insists herpetologist Eric Pianka. But perception is everything, and most humans do not
look at lizards this way. Nevertheless, I suspect my friend John Netherton,
who shot all the photographs for this book, probably did—maybe not as fish,
but certainly as beautiful.

John was one of this country's premier nature photographers; he had illustrated more than twenty natural history books, including our three previous collaborations for Voyageur Press—*Frogs* (1995), *Snakes* (1999), and *Frogs:
WorldLife Library* (2000). John discovered the beauty in lizards long before I
did; in fact, I initially resisted this project when our publisher proposed it
because I failed to see much appeal in the subject. Having grown up in the
suburbs of Chicago, where lizards are about as common as grizzly bears, my
only firsthand encounters were with a few dull-colored Midwestern species
while camping in Illinois and Wisconsin. Lizards never registered on my reptilian consciousness, which responded exclusively to snakes and frogs.

John, on the other hand, grew up in Tennessee, where he encountered
greater diversity of herpetofauna. While working for the Department of Oph-
thalmology at Vanderbilt University Medical Center, where he photographed
patients' eyes in the 1970s, he began to pursue his real love in his spare time:
photographing wildlife and natural landscapes. Every spring and fall, John would
head to the Great Smoky Mountains, and, in the winter, south to the Everglades. He also began to take regular trips to other national parks, monuments,
state parks, natural areas, wetlands, mountain ranges, and deserts, eventually
extending his travels as far as South America, the Galápagos Islands, and Africa.
As a result, John had an altogether different take on lizards, and he marveled at
their singular beauty. Where I envisioned drab grays and browns and pale
stripes, John saw vivid hues and flecks and brilliant patterns. Over time, these
unsung, supposedly "noncharismatic" reptiles began to exert their own special
appeal—and John became convinced they would make a fine subject for our
next book.

Prehensile-tailed skink
*The prehensile-tailed skink, a secretive for-
est-dweller of the Solomon Islands, boasts
several curious distinctions: it is the world's
largest skink; it lives in trees, rather than on
the ground; and it has a remarkable tail
(unique among skinks) that can grasp tree
limbs for support.*

"Skinks run the gamut from
heavy-limbed types to perfectly naked torpedoes."

—*Thomas Palmer,* Landscape
with Reptile, *1992*

So I am especially saddened that John was never able to see the final published work. Just two weeks after completing the principal photography for this volume, John suffered a heart attack at his home in Nashville, Tennessee, and died at the age of fifty-two.

I was devastated. John and I had been friends for twenty-five years and collaborators for two decades. His recent books—finished and unfinished—confirm he was at the apex of his artistic powers. Since I had completed only a few chapters of this text at the time of his death, I entertained doubts about proceeding without him. But John's photographs were so gorgeous, and so joyful, it would have been unseemly not to continue. Besides, his three sons all felt this book would make a fitting tribute to their father.

The original concept was straightforward: a companion volume to *Frogs* and *Snakes*, sumptuously illustrated but nontechnical in nature, designed for general readers. John's portfolio of lizard photographs would showcase a sampling of common species familiar to many readers, as well as some unusual and exotic species from around the world. (John's many friends, including zoo curators and private collectors, provided the exotics for him to shoot.) He was able to photograph representatives of the three major lineages of lizards—Iguanians, Gekkotans, and Autarchoglossans—but had hoped to shoot a basilisk, thorny devil, flying dragon, galliwasp, and other species before he died.

Like our previous volumes, *Lizards* is not intended to be a field guide (Roger Conant and Joseph T. Collins's *Field Guide to the Reptiles and Amphibians of Eastern and Central North America* and Robert Stebbins's *Field Guide to Western Reptiles and Amphibians* cover that subject matter superbly). Instead, this book strives to showcase a variety of physical characteristics and behaviors of lizards and to explore the natural history of selected species, the curious relationship between lizards and humans, and current threats to lizard populations and their habitats. Significantly, while declining amphibian populations have received the lion's share of media attention in recent years, scientists reported in 2000 that "reptiles appear to be in even greater danger of extinction worldwide."

Herpetologists, of course, keep one another apprised of their research by publishing their findings in scholarly journals; the language and complexity of these articles, however, can frustrate readers without scientific backgrounds. Accordingly, we endeavor here to communicate directly with the public at large, to help them better

Eastern glass lizard
The Eastern glass lizard, found in coastal regions of the southern United States, is related to the even larger Scheltopusik lizard of southeastern Europe and Central Asia. These unusual lizards have spawned numerous myths, due to their uncanny resemblance to snakes.

Parson's chameleon
The shy but beautiful Parson's chameleon, found in the cool rain forest canopy of eastern Madagascar, may be the world's largest species of chameleon.

understand and appreciate these creatures with inspiring photography and text that unites information from popular literature with material from scholarly sources.

"Few people live in the parts of the country where lizards abound, and vice versa," herpetologist Clifford H. Pope wrote in 1956. "In the East, lizards are less abundant and much less conspicuous. The hopeless confusion of lizards with the innumerable salamanders of our Eastern woodlands adds greatly to the lack of clear thinking about lizards."

Clear thinking about lizards is, of course, always commendable. (Actually, any thinking about lizards is probably a good sign.) Lizards are the largest extant group of reptiles, but they have not yet entered the collective consciousness in the manner of serpents or crocodilians. Popular culture offers us an occasional glimpse—the Budweiser chameleons, GEICO geckos, SoBe lizard beverages, motion picture Godzillas, even Orlando's cityscape "LizArt." But lizards remain a fairly well-kept secret—except among the legions of pet owners who have boosted reptiles into the ranks of the pet trade's most popular animals.

Since agreeing to undertake this project, I have chased Sierra fence lizards in Yosemite National Park, startled squadrons of Cuban brown anoles in Florida parks, ogled monitors and crocodile lizards at the San Diego Zoo, accompanied my friend and patient colleague Brian Miller on field trips with his students to collect herps in the cedar glades of Tennessee, observed basilisks and prehensile-tailed skinks at the California Academy of Sciences, patted the head of an enormous but amiable rhinoceros iguana at the Nashville Zoo, and cohabited with a green anole that tolerated my voyeuristic scrutiny. Mostly, however, I spent hours in the university library, searching for interesting facts and anecdotes to enliven the text that would eventually accompany John's photos.

Although, due to his untimely death, I was unable to record John's tales of how he secured his favorite lizard photographs, I can share one personal anecdote. On a midday visit to John at his home adjoining his beloved Radnor Lake State Natural Area, I found him preoccupied with shooting intimate close-ups of flowers (his "Georgia O'Keeffes," he liked to call them). Somewhat hesitantly, I inquired when he was going to shoot some more *lizard* pictures. He deftly changed the subject, but as we stepped outside his porch onto his patio, he glanced up at his roof and pointed. There, believe it or not, was a five-lined skink on some leaf litter in his gutter, peering down at us.

"Don't worry," John chuckled, raising his "Lizard Lick, N.C." cap in a gesture of solidarity, or perhaps a salute. "If I don't find the lizards, then I guess the lizards will just find me."

15

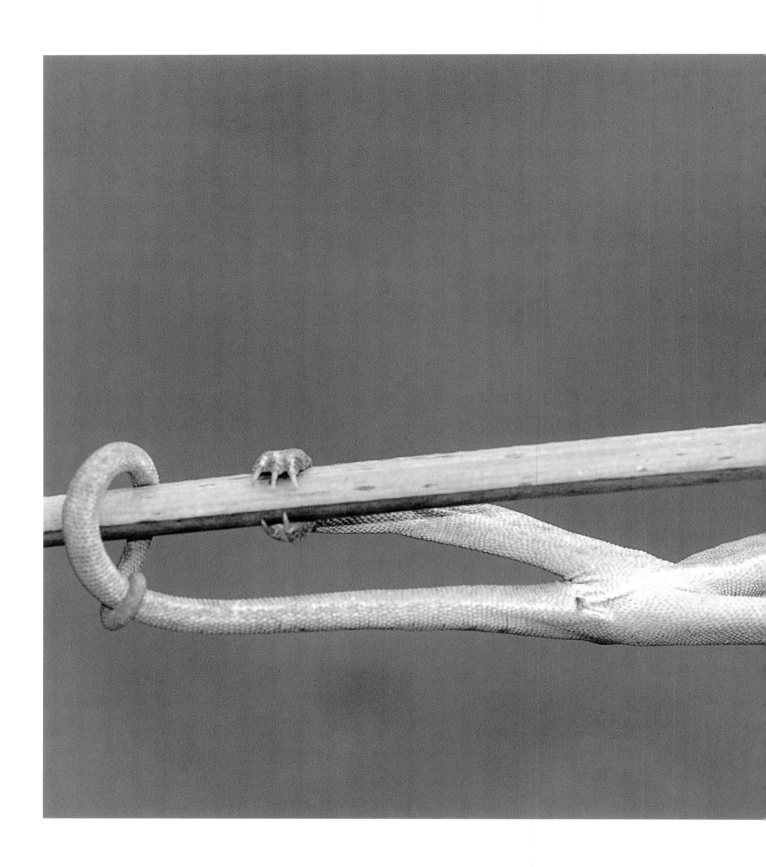

Senegal chameleon

The smooth-skinned Senegal chameleon of West Africa secures a firm grip on branches with its bundled toes and prehensile tail. Although one of the most popular imported species, this chameleon seldom does well in captivity, due to problems with internal parasites.

Chapter 1

Lizards and Humans

"The human imagination has never run as wild with lizards as it has with snakes," Clifford Pope once opined. Indeed, the Bible, ancient myths, fairy tales, folklore, and popular culture have generally featured serpents (invariably malevolent ones) instead of lizards. But lizards have not been entirely ignored—in fact, they could very well be the prototypes for Eastern and Western dragons.

According to some science writers and folklorists, the original model for the Chinese dragon was probably a lizard. "There is a good deal more monitor lizard than crocodile in the stylish, coiled dragon of Chinese legends," notes herpetologist Robert Sprackland. Others, however, speculate that dinosaur bones are responsible for legends of giant dragons (the word *dinosaur* means "terrible" or "fearfully great lizard").

"Mankind has long had a fascination with giant reptiles," declares Sprackland, pointing out that the early taxonomist Carolus Linnaeus bestowed the name *Draco* on the East Asian gliding agama "because, upon seeing their wings, he was convinced that these were the hatchlings of the giant dragons he had heard about." Clever forgers, in fact, manufactured baby "dragons" during the sixteenth century by stitching bat wings onto the bodies of lizards.

Because of their physical resemblance, lizards have doubled for dinosaurs throughout much of Hollywood history, dating as far back as *On Moonshine Mountain* (1914). In *One Million B.C.* (1940) and its sci-fi descendants, lizards were often dressed up with cardboard fins to give them a more "authentic" dinosaur look.

Godzilla, the reptilian megastar of sixteen films since his 1956 debut, is probably the "best-known cinematic lizard of all," according to *Loco for Lizards* author Jim Cherry. Another hulking villain is the star of *The Giant Gila Monster* (1959), the saga of an atomic mutant that terrorizes Southwestern trailer courts. In *The Freshman* (1990), a Godfather-like Marlon Brando hires Matthew Broderick to procure a rare Komodo dragon for his endangered-species gourmet club, and in *Komodo* (2000) a youngster faces down surly monitors that have feasted on his family.

Veiled chameleon
Found on dry plateaus and rocky steppes of Yemen and southwestern Saudi Arabia, the brightly colored veiled chameleon sports a remarkable casque atop its head that scientists believe may have evolved to collect dew or to store fat.

"The chameleon in the hotel court. He is fat and indolent and contemplative, but is businesslike and capable when a fly comes about. . . . He is always pious, in his looks. . . . He has a froggy head, and a back like a new grave—for shape; and hands like a bird's toes that have been frost-bitten."

—*Mark Twain,* Following the Equator, *1897*

Marine iguana

The Galápagos Islands are home to the marine iguana, the world's only "oceangoing" lizard. Although accorded protection from the swarms of tourists that visit the island, marine iguana colonies are threatened by oil spills from tankers that have run aground on nearby reefs.

Perhaps the most unusual lizard film is director Woody Allen's *Zelig* (1983), a mock documentary about "human chameleon" Leonard Zelig, who can transform himself into other people. In due time, Zelig becomes a folk hero and inspires four hit songs: "Doin' the Chameleon," "Chameleon Days," "Leonard the Lizard," and "Reptile Eyes." And in director Oliver Stone's *Wall Street* (1987), a slimy financier played by Michael Douglas is given the reptilian name Gordon Gekko.

Lizards surface sporadically in literature too, especially in children's books. Marjorie Sharmat's *Gila Monsters Meet You at the Airport* relates the anxieties of a young New Yorker about to move out West, where, he is warned, he will be confronted by repulsive reptiles. Hanne Türk's *Hieronymus* is about an African chameleon who uses his color-changing talents to great advantage; Bruce Hale's *Chet Gecko* detective series is about a gumshoe gecko; Tony Johnston's *The Iguana Brothers* features siesta-prone siblings who dream of being dinosaurs; and Daniel Pinkwater's *Lizard Music* features a lad with "lizards on the brain" who finds adventure among music-loving lizards.

Elsewhere in popular culture, musicians have christened their musical groups with lizard names—including the Austin Lounge Lizards, Munich Lounge Lizards, Swing Lizards, Flying Lizards, Beach Lizards, Grinning Lizards, Fancy Lizards, Thundering Lizards, Leapin' Lizards, Lizard Train, Horny Toads, and Big Nick and the Gila Monsters. Rock star Iggy Pop acquired his name when he played drums for The Iguanas, and Jim Morrison of The Doors relished the erotic appeal of his nickname "The Lizard King."

Lizards have been tapped to promote beer (laid-back chameleons Frank and Louie supplanted the Budweiser bullfrogs in TV ads), insurance, beverages, running shoes, even teeth-whiteners. They also appear on postage stamps, T-shirts, caps, jewelry, doormats, software, plush animals, rubber toys, and art—including Native American pottery and leatherwork. "Lizards," concludes Cherry, "have insinuated themselves deeply into our culture, as stealthily as a hungry chameleon eyeing its prey."

Myths and traditions involving lizards date back thousands of years. The Egyptians, for example, carved Nile monitors on monuments, preserved desert lizards as mummies, and carried lizard charms in small boxes. The Romans sometimes depicted the messenger Mercury (Hermes in Greek mythology) in a chariot pulled by a lizard.

In Australia, Aborigines who dreamed they had been transformed into lizards created lizard totems to attain supernatural knowledge and power over the species. According to Aboriginal legend, two monitor species acquired their colors by painting each other: the perentie painted the smaller black-headed monitor with beautiful rosette patterns, but the latter tired of its more extensive task and "finished up by just throwing its bucket of paint on the back half of the perentie," Pianka recounts.

Chameleons are the subject of many myths, especially in Africa. Zulus believe the sky god sent a chameleon to humankind bearing the message of eternal life; on the way, the chameleon stopped to eat, so the animal bearing the message of death arrived first. To compensate humans for the loss of immortality, the sky god instituted marriage, "so that people's lives were carried on through their children," anthropologist Anthony Mercatante explains.

In another rendering, God decided men should come to life again after dying and dispatched the chameleon to convey the good news. "But while the reptile was crawling to deliver its message, God changed his mind and sent the lizard," who announced that God now wished men to die outright, J. G. Frazer writes. "The bearer of this gloomy intelligence outstripped the laggard chameleon, so that when the gospel messenger at last came panting in with tidings of a joyful resurrection, nobody would believe him, and both reptiles were knocked on the head . . . the lizard for coming in first with bad news and the chameleon for coming in second with good." In another tale, God sent a chameleon, frog, and bird as messengers to humans, but the chameleon "bungled" his task, so God "degraded him" and made him walk slowly, Frazer relates, "lurching to and fro before every step."

In a Rhodesian version, God put men on earth, then decided to call them back to make them all different. Messenger animals were sent to far-reaching populations, but the chameleon "delayed so much that the black man, to whom it had been sent, arrived only in time to receive the poorest of all the gifts," Pope recounts. "In his anger, this wretched victim put a curse upon the chameleon; forevermore its kind would move no more rapidly than did that messenger."

Impressed by the chameleon's ability to change color, some Europeans believed it could assume the shape of an object it approached. They also supposed this lizard fed entirely on air (hence Hamlet's remark in the Shakespeare play: "Of the chameleon's dish: I eat the air, promise-crammed"). In Tuscany and Sicily, the green lacerta lizard

Marbled gecko
The marbled gecko, named for its dark-brown or black spots, is a tree-dwelling species of southern Thailand and the Indo-Australian Archipelago. It is often found in houses, where it is attracted by roaches, crickets, and small mice.

is considered the friend of mankind and reportedly hisses in the ear of a sleeping Christian should a deadly serpent approach.

In Southeast Asia, the tokay gecko is considered a sign of good fortune and fertility; if this gecko barks shortly after a baby is born, that child is said to be blessed with a happy life. The fire skink (or Fernand's lizard), on the other hand, is believed to be a bad omen, and Africans abandon their plans for the day if they see one. Pakistanis "particularly dislike" agama lizards, according to Sherman and Madge Minton, because the characteristic head bobs and push-ups are viewed as "a mockery of their prayers."

In Madagascar, killing a chameleon is considered *fady*, or taboo, and brings bad luck. "In the north, many believe that any injury you inflict on the tiny *Brookesia* chameleon will soon happen to you," author James Martin relates. It is *fady* to eat chameleons; women must never handle them; and if a man comes in contact with one, "his wife won't let him touch her for three days," Martin says.

Native Americans depicted lizards in pictographs and petroglyphs on rock walls (including a notable "racing lizard" in New Mexico) and believed Gila monsters were medicine men who spoke directly to the Storm Spirit and could predict rain. Near Milwaukee, Wisconsin, an unknown tribe built a lizard effigy 250 feet long (76.2 m), preserved today in Lizard Mound County Park.

In North Carolina, a tiny hamlet acquired the name Lizard Lick after the federal government built a liquor still there in the late 1800s to combat local bootleggers. According to Mayor Charles Woods, the still had a rail fence on which "hundreds of lizards would run to catch insects attracted by the mash used to make whiskey." After the official whiskey taster sampled each day's run "and was feeling no pain, he would take his walking cane and run the lizards off the fence as he left for home. He called his cane the Lizard Licker."

In neighboring South Carolina, legend has it that a 7-foot (2.1-m) monster covered in green scales known as Lizard Man inhabits a local swamp. This large, squishy creature allegedly lunged out of the woods at a seventeen-year-old who was changing a tire and gave chase at speeds of up to 30 miles (48 km) per hour. Media coverage in 1988 spawned claims of additional sightings, as well as an

Blue-tailed day gecko

Geckos, such as this Madagascan blue-tailed day gecko, exhibit an extraordinary ability to cling to surfaces even when upside down, inspiring scientists to compare the microscopic bristles on their toe pads to Velcro.

abundance of bumper stickers, T-shirts, and other souvenirs. (Regional folklorists then discovered earlier legends about ferocious "lizard men" with webbed feet and scales who "terrorized" Native Americans living along the Carolina coast before the arrival of Europeans.)

Over the centuries, humans have discovered many ways to exploit lizards. In some countries, monitors are a source of meat and eggs. Aborigines consider goannas "a sort of free hamburger," Pianka reports, although Karl Schmidt and Robert Inger, who sampled monitors in Borneo, compare the meat to "very old and tough roosters." Green iguanas are a popular delicacy in Central and South America, brought to market still alive but grotesquely bound by their leg muscles. However, the Galápagos land iguana, Charles Darwin once wrote, yields a "white meat" that is liked "only by those whose stomachs soar above all prejudices."

In the Middle East, skinks are hunted for their flesh and served roasted or pulverized. Spiny-tailed lizards, served with the thorny skin removed, are also popular. In North America, native peoples relished the meat of the chuckwalla, but Whit Gibbons reports that inquisitive colleagues who sampled fried blue-tailed skinks at a Herp Dinner suddenly took ill and fled the room.

Some skinks are believed to have medicinal powers, and the Roman scholar Pliny noted that skinks were used as an antidote for wounds from poisoned arrows. Count de la Cepede, on the other hand, berated his fellow Europeans for imagining that skinks could "restore exhausted vigor and rekindle the fires of love" when employed as an aphrodisiac for the "vile purpose of disgracing the noblest of the natural passions." The oil of large monitor lizards is sold to treat failing eyesight, their flesh is considered a cure for vomiting, and tail fat is sometimes applied as a poultice or burn medicine. In the Near East, excrement of the agama was once highly prized as a cosmetic.

The skins of lizards—particularly large ones, such as monitors—are a source of leather in many parts of the world. Hundreds of thousands of tanned lizard skins are shipped from Asia and Africa each year to make boots, belts, wallets, watchbands, handbags, and even drumheads. Other lizards are stuffed and mounted.

Yet the greatest demand today for lizards is as pets. Zookeepers have long known that reptiles are a popular attraction, but snakes and lizards (reportedly the fastest-growing area of the pet trade) are particularly desirable among private collectors. Many lizards are bred in captivity, but others are imported in direct violation of U.S. laws and international treaties. In September 2000, for example, a Las Vegas man was convicted of smuggling a dozen lizards—including a Nile monitor, water monitor, and several geckos—into the United States in his underwear.

The pleasures of owning and breeding lizards are widely extolled among herpetoculturists, although pet dealers concede that thousands of imported reptiles die each year from dehydration or starvation while awaiting delivery to pet shops or buyers. According to the Royal Society for Prevention of Cruelty to Animals, "Out of every ten lizards, only one or two survive the journey." Certain varieties, such as chameleons, do poorly in captivity and have alarmingly short life spans. Health officials in the United States and Britain report cases every year of individuals, including children, who are infected with salmonella as a result of contact with "household reptiles." Owners are urged to wash their hands thoroughly with antibacterial soap after handling herps and to keep reptiles away from kitchens and surfaces where food is stored and served.

"The new vogue for reptile pets," herpetologist Archie Carr writes, "is part bravado." That may be true, but there is a status component too: blue-tongued skinks and green iguanas have been called "yuppie designer pets." In fact, many owners acquire geckos, anoles, and skinks because they find them to be attractive, pleasant, low-maintenance companions. The director of the Zurich Zoo kept an Indian monitor so tame it would swim beside him in the sea, and President Theodore Roosevelt, famous for his love of pets, once kept a lizard named Bill in the White House.

Not all lizards make suitable pets, of course, as Delaware police learned in January 2002, when they discovered the remains of a man who let his seven pet Nile monitors have run of his apartment. These lizards, which ranged in length from 2 to 6 feet (0.6 to 1.83 m), had been feeding on his body, perhaps after he had already died from unrelated causes. Curiously, the *Philadelphia Inquirer* reported, news of the incident sparked "a mad nationwide rush to buy the feisty, dangerous animals."

Fire skink

The bright crimson flanks and upper jaw of the fire skink, a forest-living species from West Africa, inspire awe and fear among some natives, who believe the vivid red colors warn of venom or some other danger.

Galápagos land iguana
When naturalist Charles Darwin encountered Galápagos land iguanas on his historic expedition to the Galápagos Islands in 1835, he described them as "ugly animals" with a "singularly stupid appearance."

Chapter 2

Physical Characteristics and Behavior

Shape and Size

"To the lizard, unequaled among other reptiles in variation of structure," Pope wrote in 1956, "variety of form and function is the spice of life." Although many lizards assume the "traditional" saurian shape and form—long, slender, and usually cylindrical, with four legs and a tail like a salamander, or stout and thicker bodied—others depart from the norm. Horned lizards, for example, are squat like toads, while iguanas and certain other species look like diminutive dinosaurs—which explains their use as "stand-ins" for dinosaurs in Hollywood movies. Furthermore, glass lizards and slow worms lack legs altogether and are frequently mistaken for snakes.

Besides variety of shape, which generally correlates with locomotion and lifestyle, lizards display a curious array of accoutrements on their head, neck, back, and tail. Chameleons and water dragons, for example, sport crests—modified or enlarged scales—on the head and back. These spiny protuberances on the skull sometimes bulge forward "like the bow of a ship" or curve "like a scythe," Martin observes in his natural history of chameleons. Somewhat more startling are the prominent conelike horns found in trios on Jackson's and Johnston's chameleons, in pairs on mountain chameleons, or as one on rhinoceros iguanas and horned agamas.

On Australian frilled lizards, flamboyant neck appendages flare out suddenly when these creatures seek to bluff their rivals or warn off attackers, while bearded dragons and many other agamids inflate their throats and display beardlike fringes of skin when harassed. Another neck appendage is the dewlap, or throat fan, which anoles and some iguanas exhibit prominently and colorfully during courtship and so-called aggression displays. Lizard feet and toes differ, too, from the minute hairlike bristles on gecko and anole toes to the long, birdlike claws of tree monitors.

Smallwood's giant anole
Anole lizards have streamlined bodies, pointed heads, and long tails that are generally twice as long as their head-body length. Anoles vary considerably in size, from smaller species to "crown supergiants" such as this Smallwood's giant anole, a native of Cuba.

"Ivy grows with strong stems up the rocks, and spreads itself wide over them, the lizard glides through the intervals, and everything that wanders to and fro reminds me of the loveliest pictures of art."

—Henry David Thoreau, A Week on the Concord and Merrimack Rivers, 1849

Lizards also vary widely in size. A Komodo dragon that measured 10¼ feet (3.1 m) from its head to the tip of its tail holds the most widely accepted record length, but authority Robert Sprackland notes a possible record of 13.2 feet (4 m) for a crocodile monitor. Walter Auffenberg, the world's leading expert on Komodos, has encountered unsubstantiated claims that Komodo dragons achieved lengths of 14 feet (4.27 m) in New Guinea and 15 to 21 feet (4.57 to 6.4 m) elsewhere. Fossil remains of an extinct Australian monitor, *Megalania prisca*, have been found that measure more than 19½ feet (6 m); this creature, marvels naturalist David Quammen, "wasn't a dinosaur, it wasn't a crocodile—it was a *lizard*."

At the opposite end of the scale are some very tiny lizards, the smallest of which, the dwarf gecko (*Sphaerodactylus ariasae*), is also the world's smallest reptile. Discovered in 2001 on Isla Beata off the coast of the Dominican Republic, this endangered species is just six-tenths of an inch (16 mm) in length and can curl up on a coin the size of a dime.

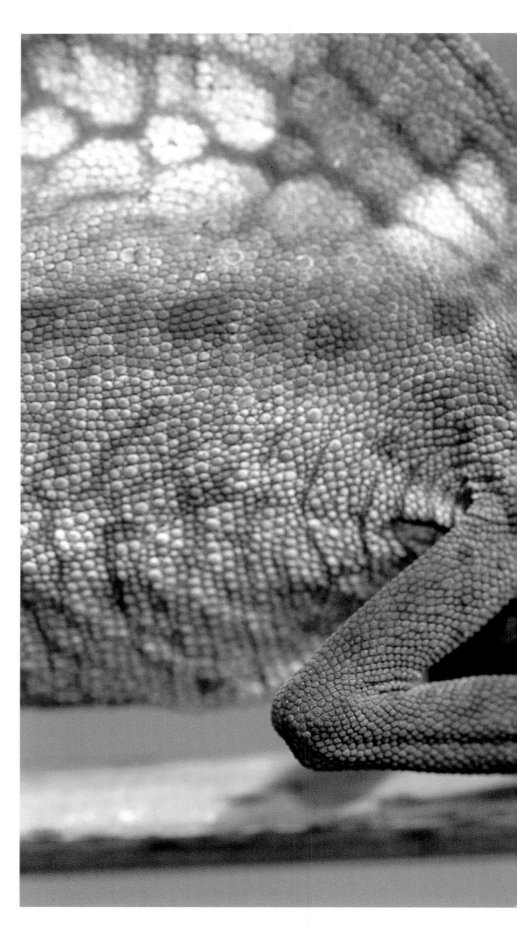

Crested chameleon
Many species of chameleons, such as this crested or sailfin chameleon from West Africa, have flaps, helmets, or casques on or behind the head, as well as bony ridges of scales, called combs or crests, that extend down the head and back.

Asian green water dragons

Asian green water dragons are long, slender lizards whose tails may constitute two-thirds of their total body length. Water dragons commonly bask on tree limbs overhanging rivers and lakes, and they are proficient divers and swimmers.

Skin and Coloration

The outer skin of a lizard, like that of a snake, is covered with protective scales that are dry to the touch and differ significantly in appearance and arrangement among species. The thickened outer skin of some is horny and coarse, with rows of spiny protuberances or plates that offer protection from enemies and help to prevent moisture and heat loss. Other lizards, such as geckos, can have soft overlapping scales (like roof tiles) or nodules, which have a velvety or tissuelike appearance. Skinks, on the other hand, have smooth, shiny scales that look as if they have been polished. As lizards grow, they periodically shed their outer epidermal covering—usually in pieces and flakes, rather than in a single piece like most snakes.

Unlike frogs and salamanders, which have water-permeable skin that functions as a respiratory membrane, most lizards have thicker skin that is sometimes reinforced with bony plates and contains few glands. According to herpetologist Raymond Ditmars, some desert species of spiny-tailed lizards with especially coarse or granular scales may absorb liquid nourishment through their skin. Other authorities note that Gila monsters have "leaky skins" and therefore remain underground much of the summer to prevent excessive moisture loss.

When a lizard "sheds" its skin, it doesn't slough its only covering. These reptiles actually have three layers: the epidermis, or outer skin; the dermis, which consists of connective tissues, membranes, blood vessels, nerves, and cells that affect color; and the subcutis, or lower skin, which anchors the skin to the muscles below.

Shedding, which is more frequent among juveniles than among adults, usually takes place shortly after hatching and at irregular intervals, depending upon temperature, moisture, food supply, growth, and general health. A lizard often endeavors to speed the process of shedding by pulling the outer skin with its mouth or scratching with its feet and claws. Some lizards (like some frogs) eat the rejected skin as they peel the flakes off their body.

After the sections of old skin, or individual scales of larger species, have been shed, the new epidermis shines brightly and affords a fine display of the lizard's true colors. Sometimes when the outer skin of an anole flakes and splits down the middle of the back, the lizard looks as if it has sprouted moth wings, while chameleons may look as if they have been wrapped in white tissue paper. Just as some frogs and salamanders will initiate the shedding process by "popping" their eyes to stretch their skin, some lizards will bulge their eyes and loosen the neighboring skin by contracting muscles and forcing blood into a system of sinuses in their head.

Some geckos even rely on their skin-shedding talents to help them escape from predators. Quammen notes that the island-dwelling *Gehyra mutilata* is one of a handful of geckos that engage in "shock-shedding"—casting off their entire skin when handled or grabbed and slipping away all "pink and naked and raw." According to gecko authorities Friedrich-Wilhelm Henkel and Wolfgang Schmidt, this unusual defensive behavior triggers minimal bleeding and apparently causes no injury to the gecko. The skin of other geckos is sometimes so transparent that it is possible to count the eggs in a pregnant female from the outside.

The prominent ornamentation on many lizards actually consists of enlarged, odd-shaped scales; conspicuous examples include the horns on Jackson's and sail-finned chameleons, the spiked dorsal crests on iguanas and agamids, and the flamboyant ruff on a frilled lizard. Bearded dragons sport an array of sharp, pointed scales along their throat; horned lizards and thorny devils are equipped with rows of smaller spines on their head and flanks; and spiny-tailed lizards have sharply pointed scales on their short, clublike tails. Flying dragons of Southeast Asia have large flaps of skin along the sides of the body that permit them to glide from trees, and anoles and iguanas have folds of skin (dewlaps) hanging from the throat that spread like fans to warn intruders and advertise the lizard's sex.

Skin colors and patterns of lizards are especially important as communication cues because, herpetologist Chris Mattison explains, "lizards are the most visually oriented of the reptiles." Although the brighter, bolder colors of males are often characterized as "nuptial colors" intended to attract the opposite sex, authority Hobart Smith argues that the real function of an anole's bright red (or yellow or purple) dewlap, or the bright blue on the throat or flank of a chuckwalla, is not to attract females "but rather to send other competitors or enemies away." Accordingly, these often vivid colors and striking patterns require a well-developed sense of vision, rather than the well-developed sense of hearing that frogs and toads exhibit when courting.

The colors of lizards, particularly those of color-changing chameleons, anoles, and geckos, are especially attractive to hobbyists and breeders. Of the quick-change artists, chameleons are probably the best known but also among the least understood, since most people believe chameleons alter their colors to blend in with their surroundings. Color change for chameleons and certain other lizards is not a disguise, Martin explains, but rather a way to make the chameleon "more conspicuous" in courtship or in response to threats—the change in color is essentially a form of communication.

Fat–tailed gecko
Unlike most snakes, lizards characteristically shed their skin in patches and pieces. This captive-bred fat-tailed gecko, a species native to Africa, will reveal brighter skin coloration and patterns after shedding its old coat of skin.

"At other times the things I have learned and the things I have been taught drop away, as the lizard sheds its skin."

—*Helen Keller,* The Story of My Life, *1902*

Researchers have identified eight significant variables that can affect the color of a lizard. As enumerated by Smith, these include: (1) age or stage of growth; (2) gender; (3) color of the environment; (4) season of the year; (5) temperature; (6) mood or state of excitement; (7) physical state of health; and (8) intensity of light.

While some changes in color are voluntary, others are strictly involuntary, as close observation of the sleeping habits of chameleons and anoles reveals. In the morning, for example, when temperatures are still cool, many lizards assume a darker shade of color to absorb radiant heat. Then, if the temperature becomes too hot, the dark color "suddenly changes to a quite light one," explains herpetologist Robert Mertens, to avoid "heating beyond the optimum." During courtship, a male chameleon adopts his flashiest colors and bobs his head repeatedly to signal his gender to a prospective mate or to warn off a rival suitor. A startled chameleon may suddenly turn black with anger or exhibit a pattern of spots and stripes—sometimes in less than a minute.

Anole lizards (mistakenly called "chameleons" in Florida and other Southern states) are famous for their quick transformation from bright green to brown and then back again. Bright green is the "activity color," explains researcher Hilda Simon, displayed "when the animal feels insecure, endangered, or uncomfortable, as well as during periods of exertion." Brown, the "response color," signals that the anole is "comparatively calm, tranquil, or sleepy, regardless of the color of its background." As for camouflage, color phases "may very well have a protective value," she says, "not so much because of the animal's background, but because of its own condition."

When a chameleon changes color, pigment-bearing cells (called chromatophores) beneath the lizard's transparent skin either expand or shrink. These cells, which contain red and yellow pigment, are modified when other cells, which reflect blue and white or contain dark-brown melanin, mix or mask the brightly colored cells and thus darken their hues. Droplets of yellow pigment under an anole's outer layer of skin fill spaces between other cells; when deeper layers of white cells reflect blue light back through the yellow layer, the lizard's skin color changes to green.

Some members of another family, the agamids of Asia and Africa, can change color as strikingly as chameleons. "I witnessed the fascinating transformation of a reptilian Cinderella," Simon wrote of one such agamid. This mottled brown-and-gray specimen suddenly turned bright turquoise on the head and neck, and jade green on its back, when its terrarium was placed on a radiator and exposed to winter sun. Force-feeding accelerated the color change, and eventually a pattern of reddish-brown spots and cream-colored stripes "stood out like a gem-studded necklace," and the throat patch turned deep violet and purple.

Panther chameleon skin
A close-up view of the skin of a panther chameleon reveals enlarged scales, called tubercles, of different sizes and colors. When influenced by temperature, disposition of the animal, and other variables, chameleon skin color can change rapidly.

Crocodile monitor skin
The skin of a crocodile monitor consists of smooth, overlapping polygonal-shaped scales. Natives of Papua New Guinea, where this monitor is found, use its skin to make drumheads.

Facing page:
Lined leaf-tailed gecko
The cryptic coloration and patterns of a lined leaf-tailed gecko and the lizard's streamlined shape camouflage this Madagascan species when it perches on the bark strips of a tree.

> "It is not usually necessary to go out looking for geckos—they make house-calls, and are the ultimate lounge-lizards."
>
> —*Chris Mattison,* Lizards of the World, *1989*

Blue-tailed day gecko
The blue-tailed day gecko is one of the world's most brilliantly colored lizards. Visitors to Madagascar and the island of Mauritius marvel at this day gecko's neon-bright turquoise and green colors with rows of deep-red spots as it climbs palms and banana trees and perches conspicuously on fences and walls.

Limbs and Locomotion

"When it comes to ways of getting about, lizards are in a class by themselves," Pope once observed. In addition to the usual repertoire of reptilian locomotive techniques—walking on four legs, swimming, climbing, and burrowing—lizards have evolved some other, more unusual skills: gliding from trees, flinging their bodies into the air, "swimming" through sand, running on water, and walking upside down across a ceiling. That's real versatility.

The "typical" lizard walks on four legs; some rely on thick but relatively short limbs, others on longer, spindly limbs. These four legs are what Smith calls the "expected accouterments" of lizards, although a number of families sport no external limbs at all or have only two. Hands and feet generally have five toes, with the fourth digit on the foot (and usually the hand) longer than the others. When sleeping, anoles and geckos often stretch out their long hind legs and point them toward the rear, rather like a weary hound that has collapsed flat on its stomach.

Lizards with four legs have mastered the art of outrunning most predators, including humans, as anyone who has ever chased an anole or skink can attest. Since their very survival may depend on their speed, the swift flitting, dashing, and darting of lizards have attracted human attention. Collared and zebra-tailed lizards have been clocked at an impressive 16 to 17 miles (26 to 27 km) per hour, and the six-lined racerunner has been timed for short distances at 18 miles (29 km) per hour. Lizards are "the fastest-moving of all North American reptiles," according to herpetologist Will Barker.

To achieve top speeds, some lizards (e.g., collared lizards and basilisks) can run on their hind legs alone, "an old stunt for reptiles," says Pope, that recalls the stance of museum-display dinosaurs. Other species, such as the South American tegus, leap into the air and use their tail to fling themselves forward. Well-developed claws enable some lizards to climb easily, while others, like a few varieties of frogs and snakes, have developed the ability to "parachute" or glide through the air. The flying dragon of tropical rain forests spreads its winglike membranes, "runs forward a short distance, leaps into the void . . . and floats away," Mertens recounts. Other gliding lizards, such as the parachute and leaf-tailed geckos, have broad tails and webbing between their toes that slow their descent when parachuting for short distances.

Equally amazing is the so-called Jesus Christ lizard of Central and South America, a basilisk celebrated for its ability to walk—actually, to skim—across water. Scientists who have studied films of this lizard say the secret to its success is the unique way it slaps the water with its feet, which have a fringe of skin surrounding the toes.

"As the foot crashes down," James Glasheen and Thomas McMahon report, "it pushes water molecules aside and creates potholes of air. . . . The lizard obtains support from forces created by the difference in pressure between the air above the foot and the hydrostatic pressure below." The combined slap and stroke produce more than sufficient support to keep the lizard on the surface, but, if the basilisk fails to pull its foot out of the "pothole" of air quickly enough, the lizard will sink.

As for geckos, some have extraordinary toepads that allow them to walk upside down across the ceiling of a room. Their toes were once thought to have suction disks, but scientists employing powerful microscopes have recently detected flaps of skin, called lamellae, which have millions of tiny hairlike bristles at the fringes. The tip of each bristle has thousands of slightly curved pads, totaling several billion in all. Researchers calculate that a single gecko can hold onto about 90 pounds (41 kg) of weight, thanks to an intermolecular attraction known as van der Waals force. Schmidt and Inger recall that youngsters in Malaysia would swipe hats off the heads of passersby by hanging geckos on strings from windows or rooftops; the bristles on the toes would cling to the hats, and the boys would reel in their catch.

The feet of chameleons are unusual, too, as the toes on each foot are fused into two opposing "bundles." Schmidt and Inger compare these V-shaped feet to "clasping tongs," and Carr remarks these highly efficient twig-graspers resemble "the jaws of pliers." The front feet have three toes merged on the inside and two on the outside, while the rear feet "have the opposite arrangement," Martin explains. On the ground, he adds, these ordinarily arboreal creatures "walk on the tips of their claws, like reptilian pianists playing octaves."

Leopard lizard
Named for its prominent dark spots, the leopard lizard of the American West and Southwest often startles humans by running with its front legs raised off the ground.

Lined leaf-tailed gecko
Arboreal geckos such as this lined leaf-tailed gecko are superb climbers and can ascend trees with great ease and speed. The toes and fingers of geckos vary considerably from species to species; most have clinging hairs, or bristles, that adhere to surfaces, as well as fixed or retractable claws.

Far right:
Crested gecko
The web-fingered, adhesive toes of this crested gecko permit the lizard to cling to all manner of surfaces and to move with re-markable speed.

Senegal chameleon
This Senegal chameleon supports itself on a narrow branch by gripping the tree limb with its pincerlike bundled toes. Although the prehensile tail can provide additional support, a chameleon often curls its tail into a spiral when it is relaxing.

Eyes and Vision

"In general," Count de la Cepede wrote in 1802, "the eyes of lizards . . . are excellent." That assessment holds true today, and scientists marvel at the unusual variety of lizard lids and pupils and, in the case of chameleons, independent eyeball rotation.

Excellent vision is not just a luxury among lizards—their very livelihood depends on it. Mattison argues that vision, which is the lizard's primary means of detecting prey and predators, is "the most important sense in all but a few lizard species."

Herpetologist Charles Bogert once observed that iguanas in the American tropics would "flee to safety when they apparently saw me coming toward them from distances of a hundred feet (30.5 m) or more." W. Frank Blair, during his intensive study of the rusty (or Texas spiny) lizard, found his wary subjects would allow dogs to approach them while basking in trees "but would run if approached by a human."

Since most diurnal (day-active) lizards can also identify colors, the bright red, yellow, orange, and even lavender dewlaps of certain anoles—as well as the vivid blue throats, tails, flanks, and tongues of other lizards—are readily apparent to rivals, intruders, and prospective mates.

To protect their eyes, lizards have developed several mechanisms. Like eyelash vipers and Asian horned frogs, crested geckos and several other lizards have evolved "eyebrows" and "eyelashes"—actually, scaly protuberances—that offer a line of defense against sand and grit. The most effective protection, however, is the eyelid, of which lizards have four main types.

"Instead of always having a glassy stare like that of snakes," Pope says, most lizards "look out between well-developed lids." These lids are opaque and movable, the lower lid moving to cover the eye opening while the upper lid remains stationary. Beneath the movable eyelid, an elastic sheet of tissue called the nictitating membrane cleanses the eye's surface. Most geckos, however, lack movable eyelids; their upper and lower lids have, in effect, fused to fashion one transparent scale, or brille, like the permanent spectacle on the eye of a snake. "In other words," explains Mattison, "the eye is 'closed' all of the time, and the lizard sees out of a window in its eyelid." Geckos keep this transparent scale free of dirt by licking it frequently with their tongue.

Another eyelid modification, present in certain skinks, rock lizards, earless lizards, whiptails, and anguids, is a "transparent window" in the movable lower eyelid that allows the lizard to "close" its eyes but continue to see. Finally, in the so-called blind lizards, scales completely cover the rudimentary eyes, which serve little purpose in an underground lifestyle.

Lizard eyes themselves can be quite striking. Many nocturnal species such as geckos have huge eyes, while others, chiefly burrowing varieties such as the California legless lizard, have very reduced eyes, sometimes mere vestiges. The eyesight of most lizards is "exceptionally good," Robert Stebbins observed in 1954, and their "lens-squeezing" mechanism for focusing on nearby objects "should be the envy of those persons who, with increasing age, have been forced to wear glasses to compensate for loss of lens elasticity."

The shape of the pupil may be round, as in many diurnal species, or vertically elliptical, as in many geckos and other nocturnal and crepuscular forms. (The vertical slit is also characteristic of crocodiles, certain snakes, the tuatara, and many frogs.) The elliptical slit in the large, globe-shaped eye of nocturnal geckos is unusual because it includes tiny pinholes—usually no more than four—visible when the pupil closes down during exposure to bright light. Until recently, the prevailing hypothesis, as explained by Schmidt and Inger, was that each pinhole intensified the image by focusing on the retina at the back of the eyeball and then superimposing the four images. In darkness, a single image might lack sufficient light to activate the visual cells, but combined light from four pinholes could stimulate the retina, they noted. Today, however, herpetologists believe that to control the amount of light entering the eye, a gecko's pupils simply open wider as lighting dims or close down when the nocturnal gecko encounters bright light, such as when it is basking in the sun.

Even more unusual than the gecko's pinhole pupils are the chameleon's independently moving eyeballs, housed in a protruding skin dome often compared to the gun turrets of a B-29. These hulking eyes, with their small

Crested gecko

The New Caledonian crested or eyelash gecko has narrow vertical pupils that control the amount of light that enters the eyes and permit this species to see well at dusk and in the dark. The "eyelash" scales offer protection for the eye, which lacks a movable lid.

peepholes, "are unique among those of vertebrates," F. Harvey Pough et al. explain, because of their exceptional mobility and independence: one eye can swivel up while the other swivels down, or one can peer forward while the other checks out the rear. Such a large field of vision (each eye can cover 180 degrees) is a real asset for this slow-moving creature, which can watch simultaneously for prey and predators without moving.

When a chameleon spots a likely meal, its eyes zero in on the target, making the lizard look cross-eyed. The eyes focus rapidly, and the lens enlarges the image on the retina—"acting like a telephoto lens to magnify a small region of the visual world," Pough et al. note. In experiments to determine whether a chameleon's ability to cal-

culate distance and snare prey is affected when vision is restricted to one eye, a Jackson's chameleon was fitted with a pair of glasses on its horns; it had nearly equal success with one eye as with two.

Many lizards harbor a rudimentary organ on top of their head known as a parietal or "third eye." In some iguanids, this "degenerated" eye actually contains a lens, cornea, retina, and nerve endings that connect to the brain. "The function of the third eye is by no means certain," Mattison says, although some scientists believe this organ may play a role in thermoregulation, coordinating and regulating exposure to solar radiation during basking and perhaps hibernation.

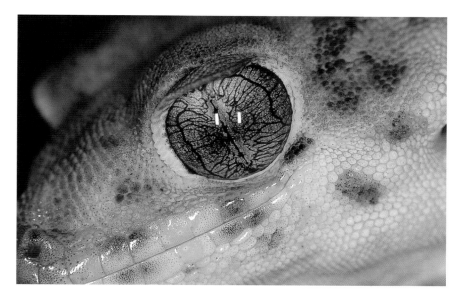

Frog-eyed gecko
A close look at the desert-dwelling frog-eyed gecko of central and southwest Asia reveals rims over the lizard's large eyes that serve as eyelashes or "winking scales." The rim protects the delicate eye from particles of sand and other objects when the gecko digs a burrow.

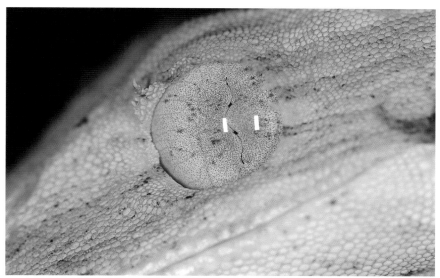

Lined leaf-tailed gecko
The narrow pupil of a lined leaf-tailed gecko has tiny pinholes that widen at night when the gecko becomes active. These pinholes intensify the amount of available light, improving the nocturnal lizard's eyesight.

Panther chameleon
The protruding eyes of chameleons such as this panther chameleon are often likened to the swiveling turret of a gun mounted on a warship or airplane. Each eye operates independently of the other, viewing 180 degrees to the side and back and judging depth with stereoscopic 3-D vision.

"The chameleons are the sharpshooters among the reptiles."

—*Karl P. Schmidt and Robert F. Inger,* Living Reptiles of the World, *1957*

Cuban false chameleon
Closely related to the anoles, the Cuban false chameleon is a large (up to 2 feet, or 61 cm) but slow-moving lizard that can move its eyes independently. Unlike chameleons and some anoles, however, it cannot change its body color.

Ears and Hearing

Lizards hear "quite well," says herpetologist Thomas Tyning, and they are responsive to "many sounds in their immediate vicinity." Unlike snakes, which have no external ear openings and respond chiefly to vibrations, most lizards have visible external openings. According to Ernest Wever, author of *The Reptile Ear*, the structure of the outer ear varies among species. In some lizards, a semitransparent tympanum lies flush with the animal's head or is only slightly depressed, while in others it rests at the end of a short vestibule. In burrowing species, an earflap often covers the exposed eardrum to protect the opening, although some species, such as the Bornean earless monitor, have no external ear openings whatsoever.

Herpetologists did not always believe that lizards could hear. In 1954, Stebbins wrote: "In general, lizards seem oblivious to sound. Even a gunshot near a basking individual may cause no outward sign of response." And for years, monitor lizards were thought to ignore sounds. One researcher who set up a blind to study Komodo dragons in their native habitat reported that neither whispers nor raised voices elicited a response from nearby monitors. Even when he tried shouting, the dragons showed no reaction.

Does that single encounter "prove" Komodo dragons are deaf? Certainly not. London Zoological Garden employee Joan Proctor was able to train a captive monitor to respond to her voice and come out to be fed—even when it could not see her approach.

Among lizards, geckos have developed a particularly fine sense of hearing; most are nocturnal and therefore rely on their ears to locate mates. Geckos produce a range of calls—from chirps and squeaks to loud barks—and without sensitive auditory organs they would have difficulty finding sexual partners. Chameleons, on the other hand, are notoriously hard of hearing, and Martin claims that even shouting beside a sleeping chameleon will not wake it up. It is possible that chameleons cannot hear sounds at higher frequencies. "Chameleons don't respond to tones much above middle C," observes Martin. "If they listened to music, they would favor works for the tuba."

Recent experiments suggest that the lateral body walls and lungs of some species of lizards may function to detect sound at low frequencies. When sound causes the body wall to vibrate, air carries the vibrations from the lungs to the inner ear, where it is processed. "While sound may get in through other routes," researcher Thomas Hetherington reports, "the lungs are clearly the most sensitive to sound waves."

Jamaican giant anole
The dark external ear opening of a Jamaican giant anole is clearly visible at the back of the head.

Leopard gecko
Nocturnal lizards such as this juvenile leopard gecko often have especially sensitive ears. Many night-active geckos communicate with calls, which require well-developed acoustic sensory organs.

Ameiva
The ameivas of Central and South America are a genus of some fourteen ground-dwelling species that are active during the day. This ameiva, photographed on the island of Bonaire, basks atop coral, where it can watch and listen for predators and prey.

Golden gecko
A lizard's tongue collects molecular cues from its environment and transports them to the Jacobson's organ for identification. Geckos also use their fleshy tongue to lap up water and to clean the transparent scale that covers each eye.

Smell and Taste

A lizard's nose functions as both a breathing organ and an external organ of smell, but this olfactory instrument isn't the animal's only means of smell. For lizards and snakes, the tongue and Jacobson's organ are the real key to olfactory success.

"Reptiles have relatively simple brains," says Lyall Watson, author of *Jacobson's Organ and the Remarkable Nature of Smell*. "In most of them, Jacobson's organ appears to provide all the information a cold-blooded animal needs to go about the daily business of finding its way about and feeding. The organ also seems to play a vital role in successful mating." Named for its discoverer, the Danish surgeon Ludwig Jacobson, this organ is a chemical sense system and "unconscious partner to the nose," explains Watson. It is also the brain's "olfactory autopilot."

The lizard's tongue, which may be short and fleshy or long and deeply forked, acquires sensory information for Jacobson's organ. The tongue flicks in and out of the mouth, picking up airborne particles and substrate cues and pressing them into a pair of dome-shaped chambers in the roof of the mouth. Sensitive cells that line these chambers assess the particles, and nerves transmit the information directly to the brain. Taste buds on the tongue and the lining of the mouth also provide sensory information.

Herpetologist Angus Bellairs observes that the tongue and Jacobson's organ perform multiple functions, including "trailing prey, testing food, sex recognition, and courtship." Ground-dwelling species apparently have evolved more responsive olfactory systems: low-slung Western whiptail lizards, for example, flick their tongues 700 times an hour because away from the ground, scents begin to disappear and a sense of smell becomes less useful.

In adult chameleons, this organ apparently has no function, but these lizards have evolved their own remarkable device: a "popgun" tongue that can shoot out one and a half times their body length (excluding tail) and snatch prey with sticky mucus on the tongue's clublike tip. This muscular tube-shaped tongue is, in effect, "a telescopic lasso," says naturalist Ken Preston-Mafham. Bunched up accordion-like on a bony throat structure, a chameleon's tongue is lightning fast, exceeding speeds of 16½ feet (5 m) per second in the extension phase. According to herpetologist Aaron Bauer, it takes less than one-hundredth of a second for the tip of the tongue to strike its prey.

Eritrean plated lizard
Plated lizards are widely distributed in semiarid regions of southern and eastern Africa, where they eat insects, spiders, flowers, leaves, fallen fruit, and berries.

Teeth and Venom

Unlike snakes, lizards cannot stretch their jaws to ingest oversized meals. Nevertheless, their mouths are well equipped with teeth, varying in shape and size according to species, which are useful for holding—and sometimes killing—their prey. The teeth are arranged in a single row along the edge of the jawbone, usually the inner surface, although a few lizards also have teeth in the roof of the mouth.

Lizard teeth are generally conical, but some are blunt and peglike. "Flat, straight, or recurved," writes Ditmars, the teeth can be "sharply pointed or terminate in queerly serrated fashion that makes each tooth like a 'bit' of some fancy drill." In general, there is very little mastication of food: "many species seize their prey, work it about in the jaws, biting it a few times, and then swallow," says Stebbins. (Chameleons are an exception; they usually chew their food.)

At birth, most lizards (excluding some geckos) are equipped with a transitory "egg tooth" projecting from the upper lip. This sharp, razorlike tooth pierces and slits the eggshell when the baby shakes its head from side to side. Within a few days, the baby sheds the egg tooth.

In Egypt and India, geckos once inspired dread because their bite was mistakenly believed to be venomous. The saliva, "a kind of thick and frothy yellow liquor which distils from its mouth, when irritated, or when it suffers any violent emotion," was considered a "mortal poison," de la Cepede wrote in 1802.

Although other perfectly harmless lizards (including five-lined skinks of the American Southeast) are feared because of superstitions they are venomous, only two species actually possess venom: the Gila monster and the beaded lizard. Unlike venomous serpents such as cobras and rattlesnakes, which inject venom through hypodermic needlelike fangs in their upper jaw, Gila monsters have glands in the lower jaw with ducts that carry venom to mucous-membrane folds near the outer edge of their lower teeth. When these lizards clamp down on their prey (or enemies) and begin chewing, venom moves through grooves in the teeth and mixes with saliva, coating the sharp teeth that deliver the puncture wounds.

Since venom is not essential for subduing its prey (chiefly rodents and small birds), herpetologists suspect the slow-moving Gila monster developed its venom apparatus as a defense mechanism. Humans "are rarely bitten unless they have either attempted to capture these venomous lizards or have handled or malhandled captives," Charles Bogert and Rafael Martín del Campo report in their classic study, *The Gila Monster and Its Allies*. The venom is neurotoxic—similar to that of cobras—but toxicologist Findlay Russell argues that the danger of an adult human dying from a bite is "slight" because Gila monsters are unable to produce sizable doses. Recent victims report suffering symptoms of shock, fainting, perspiration, vomiting, and a severe drop in blood pressure.

Nevertheless, the bite can be quite traumatic. In the 1880s, the *Arizona Sentinel* quoted a witness who claimed his companion was bitten by a Gila monster that "clung to his wrist with the tenacity of an English bulldog." Bogert and del Campo recall a Gila monster they captured near Tucson that "seized" an armrest on their car door and retained its vicelike grip "for slightly more than 15 minutes, with its teeth embedded in the fabric and layer of foam rubber beneath it."

According to Bogert and del Campo, a sixty-year-old researcher swallowed drops of diluted Gila monster venom in 1893 and recorded the following physical reactions: "I was seized with such an internal coldness from my heart as if I was being frozen to death internally. . . . Last night whilst retiring had some sharp shooting pains in my bowels, more on the left side of the abdomen, and a sharp twinging."

Black iguana

Most lizards have small teeth that are cone-shaped and arranged around the edge of the jaw. Iguanas, such as this spiny-tailed black iguana, have broadened and flattened posterior teeth, as well as cones on the cutting edge.

Gila monster
When Gila monsters chomp down on their prey, grooves in their teeth carry venom from glands in the lower gums into the puncture wounds. Humans are rarely bitten unless attempting to handle captive specimens.

Flap-necked chameleons
The prehensile tails of chameleons such as these flap-necked chameleons offer stability and support when climbing and resting on branches, because they grasp a tree limb like a fifth hand.

Tails and Autotomy

The lizard tail, Ditmars declared in 1933, is an "invaluable organ." Not just a decorative accessory, it performs at least four major functions: grasping, balancing, fat storage, and defense.

Unlike North American lizards, which do not use their tails for grasping (except perhaps occasionally to prevent falling), true chameleons and other arboreal species, such as the Solomon Islands prehensile-tailed skink, can grip objects with their tails to expedite climbing. Prehensile tails, Pianka explains, offer a sort of "fifth leg" or "fifth hand," anchoring and supporting the lizard as it ascends or descends a shrub or tree. Wrapping its strong tail around branches makes moving from perch to perch not only easier but safer.

Other lizards rely on their tails for support to provide balance or counterbalance. "In practically all U.S. lizards, the balancing function of the tail is the most important," Smith says. "Those which have lost their tails frequently run or climb clumsily. Lizards that run on their hind legs . . . for greater speed rely upon the tail to balance the uplifted fore part of the body; they are therefore incapable of such antics when deprived of their tails."

For most lizards—especially those that must hibernate during cold winter months or estivate during prolonged hot or dry periods, or those that must deal with food shortages—the tail also serves as a storage site for fats and lipids. As fat reserves, tails often assume a bulky turnip-shaped appearance, especially among Gila monsters, beaded lizards, and certain desert-living geckos.

But tails do more than stabilize, balance, and store fats—in times of trouble, the tail becomes a weapon of defense. Some species lash their tails and deliver whiplike blows; others, equipped with rows of spines down their tails, use their armor to block crevices or burrows to rebuff their enemies. And *Diplodactylus* geckos from Australia secrete a sticky, foul-smelling substance from tail glands that deters predators.

But probably the most widespread lizard survival ploy is their unusual ability to relinquish a tail when it is snatched, or even touched, by a predator—and then regenerate a new one. Scientists call this process autotomy, the self-induced separation of an appendage of the body. Tail loss is facilitated by fracture planes located within specific vertebrae; muscles that contract at the fracture plane help induce the tail to separate from the body.

Five-lined skink
The vivid blue tail of a juvenile or female five-lined skink may distract predators from the lizard's more vulnerable—and valuable—head. When a predator grabs the tail, it breaks off, allowing the skink to escape and regenerate a new tail.

Curiously, the severed tail segment often continues to wriggle and thrash about, providing a convenient distraction while the lizard escapes. In certain cases, Bellairs reports, the tail even appears to "fly off."

To prevent debilitating loss of blood, internal sphincter muscles close off the blood vessels and start to promote healing. Losing a tail has "surprisingly little effect" on a lizard, Pianka argues, "as individuals often resume basking and foraging within minutes, as if nothing had happened." Over the next few weeks, a new tail emerges from the stub, supported internally by a cartilaginous rod, rather than by a bone; the new and often thicker appendage usually assumes a slightly different color or pattern and has abnormal scalation. (In cases where the tail fragment does not completely separate from the body, the regeneration process may create a forked tail.) Curiously, some skinks later return to the site where they lost their tail and, according to Pianka, "swallow the remains of their own tail!" Although many lizards part with their tails readily, some species do not regenerate their missing appendage.

Tail loss is not without biological "costs" to the animal, however, including immediate loss of the stored fat; interference with the sense of balance, especially if the lizard is bipedal; and, for females, reduction in the number of eggs produced.

For years, the bright tail colors—blue in particular—of skinks and certain other lizards have triggered debate among herpetologists. The bright blue tails of juvenile skinks may be an "intraspecific social signal," report scientists Laurie Vitt and William E. Cooper Jr., effectively alerting adult males that the bearers are "noncompetitors" for mates. Another hypothesis is that the conspicuous blue tails are aposematic, warning predators of the appendage's distasteful or perhaps toxic properties. Residents of some Southern states believe five-lined skinks are poisonous, possibly because pets have been known to become sick after eating skink tails.

Since, to a skink, the loss of its tail (which is replaceable) is preferable to losing its life, the vivid coloration may serve to lure a predator away from the more vulnerable head or body. When the blue tail of a skink "cuts loose and goes into its frantic break-dance routine," says Carr, "it becomes by far the most conspicuous object in the vicinity" and covers the retreat of the intended victim. As juvenile skinks approach sexual maturity, their bright blue tails begin to fade; adults, especially males, sport more cryptic colors, which better conceal them from predators.

African fat-tailed gecko
Some species of lizards store reserves of fat in their turnip- or leaf-shaped tails, which they rely on during periods of hibernation or estivation, or during prolonged shortages of food.

Emerald swift

The pectoral and pelvic girdles of lizards such as the emerald swift support well-developed front and hind limbs. Inhabitants of higher elevations of Central America, emerald swifts are fast-running ground dwellers that also climb trunks of trees.

Internal Anatomy

Lizards have a lot in common with snakes, herpetologist Harry Greene points out, since snakes are believed to have evolved from "nearly limbless lizards." While the internal anatomy of these reptiles is similar to that of other vertebrates, it is somewhat modified to fit a cylindrical body structure; the lizard's skeletal system, however, differs significantly from that of snakes.

"No snake has even traces of a pectoral girdle or front limbs," Greene notes, while most lizards do—and only a few snakes show evidence of a rudimentary pelvic girdle or external hind limbs. The pectoral and pelvic girdles of a lizard's skeletal system support well-developed front and hind limbs, used for such tasks as walking, running, digging, climbing, and swimming. The skull of a lizard differs as well: it is often "highly mobile," Bauer explains, and modification of its feeding apparatus "contributes to the success of lizards as a lineage." Monitor lizards, however, have a unique adaptation that suggests a close evolutionary relationship to snakes: they can widen their throat by dropping the lower jaw.

The teeth of most lizards are short and conical, arranged in a row around the edges of the jaws. Some species have teeth on the roof of the mouth, and others have evolved incisors, canines, and molars. Some monitors have broad, flat crowns, while others have curved teeth, used for tearing their food.

Two species of lizards—the Gila monster and Mexican beaded lizard—have specialized teeth that work in conjunction with the secretion of venom from glands in the head. Yet their teeth are "poorly adapted" as a venom apparatus, Smith says, because they have only "feeble grooves" on the inner surface. Venom must seep along these grooves and work its way into puncture wounds made by chewing.

Despite the similarities of most internal organs to those of other four-limbed vertebrates, the lizards' circulatory system stands apart. The heart, once commonly described as a three-chambered system (i.e., a left and right atrium and a single ventricle), functions as a five-chambered system would. When the ventricle contracts, its single chamber divides into three compartments, Pough et al. explain. The ability to keep "oxygen-rich and oxygen-poor blood separate in the ventricle" as it passes through the heart, they suggest, "is remarkable." As in most reptiles, the blood plasma of lizards is essentially colorless, but five species of *Prasinohaema* skinks in New Guinea and the Solomon Islands have a unique blood pigment that is green.

The excretory system of reptiles is also modified: instead of excreting most urine in fluid form, lizards conserve water by producing a chalky-white waste substance in the form of uric acid. In fact, monitors and some geckos and iguanids have no urinary bladder at all. Ducts for the urinary, digestive, and reproductive systems enter a chamber known as the cloaca, where they discharge their contents for expulsion through the anus. In males, the paired reproductive organs (hemipenes) lie inverted within the base of the tail; one of the two organs is everted through the cloaca and inserted into the female's cloaca during copulation. Although lizard hemipenes lack the ostentatious array of spines found in many snakes, Smith says, some display a variety of "flounces and irregularities of contour."

Sailfin dragon
Sailfin dragons have a laterally compressed body and a very long tail. Extensions of vertebrae in the tail support the comb or sailfin, a sail-like appendage on the upper half of the tail.

Thermoregulation

"The world is a lizard's furnace," author Ellen Meloy declares in *The Last Cheater's Waltz*. Like other reptiles and amphibians, lizards were once misleadingly called "cold-blooded," a term now largely rejected because it suggests their blood is cold. A more appropriate term is ectothermic, meaning the lizard's body temperature is not internally stabilized and most body heat must be derived from the animal's surroundings.

In fact, lizards show greater diversity of thermoregulatory behavior than other reptiles. While some lizards are thermoconformers, with body temperatures roughly the same as air temperatures, others are "heliotherms," manipulating their body temperatures and keeping them stable and high by exploiting available heat sources. Since many lizards bask in direct sunlight and live in desert habitats, they are popularly believed to be able to stand temperatures considerably higher than those tolerated by other animals. Actually, Stebbins reports, "the average of the normal activity range of many lizards (98° to 100° F, or about 36° to 37° C) is close to the body temperature of man." But the upper limits of toleration, if exceeded, quickly become lethal for lizards and other animals when the body temperature reaches about 113° F (45° C). Thus, Smith says, "it is not the upper limit of toleration that is so remarkable in some lizards," but rather the preferred temperature of certain desert species, which is often perilously close to the lethal temperature.

Lizards have evolved a number of effective strategies for adjusting to the outside temperature. Many can change color, becoming darker when they are cold and lighter when they are warm, thus absorbing or reflecting rays of sunlight. Basking in direct sunlight is an efficient way to warm the body, while seeking out rocky crevices, retreating to underground burrows, and even burying part or all of the body in the sand are ways to escape extreme heat. Unfortunately, countless thousands of lizards and snakes that seek out heat-retaining asphalt pavement fall victim to humans who accidentally or deliberately drive vehicles over them.

Elevating the body off the ground is another way to reduce direct heat; some species, such as the sand-diving lizard of the Namib Desert, even balance on one front and one hind foot at a time to reduce heat transfer from hot sand and allow their feet to cool. When overheated, some geckos, iguanas, chuckwallas, and mastigures open their mouths and pant to lower their body temperature. Similarly, some monitors open their jaws and vibrate tissues in their throat, causing water to evaporate and cooling the blood that flows through the tissues. Another strategy is to seek a convective transfer of heat in water or in the air. Thus some lizards will climb a bush in search of a breeze, since air temperatures and wind velocity "change rapidly in the first half meter above the ground," Pough et al. report.

After periods of cold, many lizards seek out direct sunlight or sun-warmed rocks and substrate to warm their bodies. Marine iguanas, for example, which forage for seaweed in cold ocean waters surrounding the Galápagos Islands, warm themselves afterwards by basking in the sun and absorbing the heat that radiates from dark lava rock. To survive their long dives, these iguanas have evolved a way to slow their heartbeat to roughly half the normal rate, which limits circulation and reduces heat loss. Back on land, male marine iguanas that guard their territories against intruders have found a way to shunt excessive heat: they sit facing the sun but hold the forepart of their body off the hot ground. This exposes their underside to cool winds blowing in from the ocean, while blood vessels in the skin expand to facilitate blood flow and carry away heat.

Curiously, not all species of desert lizards drink water; while many seek droplets that collect on vegetation or the substrate, others obtain moisture from the food they consume. Australia's thorny devil has evolved its own unique method of securing water: drops of rainwater and dew collect in channels or "canals" between the pointy scales on its back and head and then drain toward the corners of its mouth.

Sand skink
This diurnal skink burrows into desert sands using its flat head, cone-shaped snout, and broad toes. The internal temperatures of sand skinks and other lizards reflect the temperature of their surroundings. These lizards risk death if they do not avoid high daytime temperatures.

Marine iguanas
After diving into cold ocean waters off the Galápagos Islands in search of algae, marine iguanas warm themselves on land by piling on top of each other, basking in the sun, and absorbing heat that radiates from fields of dark lava.

Reproduction

"The social and sexual life of lizards," herpetologists Angus Bellairs and Richard Carrington once observed, "is exceptionally interesting and complex." Lizards, for example, have developed a remarkable repertoire of courtship behaviors; males boast a paired sex organ; some females can store sperm for years; some males have "harems"; and, miraculously, females of some species reproduce asexually without any help from males. All are pretty impressive feats, yet scientists admit they know surprisingly little about the reproductive habits of many species because they are nocturnal, live in far-flung locales, or remain out of sight for most of their lives.

Courtship often requires a lizard to reveal its true colors. Particularly flashy are the dewlaps (throat fans) of anoles: red, pink, yellow, green, purple—even one that is red, white, and blue and resembles a miniature American flag. A male anole's colorful dewlap elicits instant gender recognition from others of the same species: it is a sexual cue to females and a warning signal to rival males.

Other families of lizards sport bright colors too, advertising their sexual readiness during the mating season with bright (frequently blue) streaks on their flanks, undersides, and throats. Decorative appendages include crests, nasal or forehead horns, and dangling throat pouches; a few species wave their tails to attract the attention of the opposite sex. Some geckos, chiefly nocturnal varieties, use a mating call to advertise their whereabouts.

Male lizards "put on quite a display," Carr notes, and, for maximum effect, many adopt "stereotypical" poses or body motions to call attention to themselves. Bobbing the head vigorously up and down is one common male ritual; doing "push-ups" is another. If a female is receptive and stands her ground (some species tread in place), the male will proceed to court her with nudges, licks, or a firm bite on the neck or flank—then slip the base of his tail beneath hers and insert one hemipenis into her cloaca.

Many males are "polygamists" (Blair calls them "promiscuous"), engaging in copulation with more than one female during the breeding season. Some males simply entice eligible females that wander into range; others (such as chuckwallas) operate what Mattison calls "a kind of harem system," exercising control over females that populate a specific territory. "Large tyrant males defend large territories [and] patrol their territories daily," observes researcher Bayard Brattstrom; "only the tyrant mates with the females." Some Madagascan day geckos actually form permanent relationships, and if one partner dies, "the remaining partner will not normally mate with another," Henkel and Schmidt report. According to herpetologist Edward H. Taylor, many *Draco* species (flying dragons) also mate for life.

On occasion, the object of a male lizard's affection is another male—particularly if the second male appears receptive (like a female) or is passive or unaggressive. Under such circumstances, a sexually excited male may attempt to copulate with another, although, as Bradley Greenberg and G. K. Noble point out, this is much more likely to take place in a crowded laboratory cage, and is more a sign of "failure to recognize" than it is "proof of an inherent homosexuality."

Like snakes, male lizards evert their hemipenes from within the base of the tail, as one might pop out the inverted finger of a glove. A lizard's twin genitalia are less likely to be ornamented with spines or other ornaments, although the chameleon family harbors "an exotic terrain of lips, crests, horns, scoring and papillae for sperm to traverse," Martin says.

After internal fertilization occurs, females from a majority of species lay eggs—a reproductive strategy known as oviparity. Roughly one-fifth of species give birth to living young (viviparity), and others produce eggs that hatch just prior to or at the time of laying (ovoviviparity). Most lizard eggs are leathery or hard-shelled, yet they are also permeable to moisture, without which the embryo will die; accordingly, many females lay their eggs in moist locations, such as leaf litter, rotting wood, damp soil, or sand. Temperature can affect the speed of development of the eggs (warmer temperatures foster shorter incubations), and some require considerably longer than the typical one- to two-month incubation period to hatch. Panther chameleon eggs, for example, require 240 days, and other chameleon eggs reportedly incubate for as long as thirteen months. The gestation period for *Naultinus elegans*, a

Hatchling fence lizards
Female fence lizards lay clutches of four to seventeen eggs in shallow burrows or beneath rocks, and the young hatch approximately ten weeks later. These tiny hatchlings, measuring 0.8 to 1 inch (20.6 to 25 mm) in length, emerged from their eggs in Tennessee in July.

live-bearing gecko from New Zealand, is almost one year—"probably the longest gestation of any lizard," Mattison says.

Females of some species—especially geckos—lay their eggs in communal nesting sites, perhaps when conditions are not ideal. Pope reports, for example, that 186 gecko eggs were once found in a single window shutter in Canton, China. But most female geckos lay only two eggs at a time, and sometimes only one. The largest cache of lizard eggs ever found, according to Mattison, belonged to the teiid lizard *Kentropyx calcaratus* and numbered some 800 eggs—apparently laid by "a number of females over a period of several years."

When the young hatch, they use an egg tooth to puncture the shell membrane; this tooth is discarded during the hatchling's first skin shedding. Although most females abandon their eggs immediately after laying, a few species of skinks and glass lizards remain nearby to attend their clutches, coiling their bodies around the eggs to protect them from predators. Unlike pythons, however, these lizards are not able to raise their body temperature and "incubate" their eggs. Some parent skinks nudge their eggs or pick them up in their jaws to regroup them if they find them scattered, and some geckos remain in the vicinity of their clutches to chase away other geckos that get too close. Ironically, tokay geckos that protect their eggs and guard their young after birth sometimes devour their own offspring if the hatchlings are removed and then reintroduced several days later.

When the time comes for some arboreal chameleons to lay their eggs, they descend slowly from their treetop perches and begin digging in the earth until they find damp soil. "A chameleon digs as slowly as she walks," Martin observes; "often she digs for days, returning to the safety of the branches to sleep." In captivity, he adds, females sometimes die "from the stress of egg laying."

Lizard eggs are generally white, which makes them easy for predators to spot unless laid in a well-protected spot. Some lizards therefore roll their eggs on the ground before the calcium shell has hardened to pick up bits of dirt and leaf litter that offer protective coloring.

In the desert, where most horned lizard species lay cream-colored soft-shelled eggs on or buried in the sand, the short-horned lizard is an exception: she retains her young within her body until giving birth. Then for the next two hours, "the parent labors at six-minute intervals to bring forth each toadlet," observe naturalists Lorus and Margery Milne.

In about a dozen species of geckos and lacertids, the gender of offspring may be dependent upon the temperature of the nest—as is also the case with crocodilians, many turtles, and some snakes. Among the temperature-dependent lizards, "females are produced at cooler temperatures and males at warmer ones," Pough and his coauthors report. This is exactly the opposite of the pattern in other reptiles. "Some lizards, such as iguanas, are said to be able to change sex," Sprackland reports, citing a documented sex change from male to female in African plated lizards.

Even more remarkable is the ability of some thirty species of lizards in six different families to reproduce asexually (i.e., without the female having her eggs fertilized by a male). This method of reproduction, called parthenogenesis, produces offspring (usually all female) that are clones of their mother and that share an identical genetic makeup. Some ten species of whiptail lizards from the Southwestern United States and Mexico are among the best-known parthenogenic lizards, although others have been found in Asia and elsewhere. The "advantages" for these lizards are that "every member of the population can breed, and so they increase rapidly," Mattison explains; in addition, "females do not have to find a mate, and if they wander into new territory, they can go right ahead and begin to colonise it." On the other hand, since all individuals are identical, their species will have a difficult time adapting if conditions turn unfavorable.

Although parthenogenic females do not require fertilization to reproduce, that does not mean there is no sexual behavior. Scientists use the term "pseudocopulation" to characterize the behavior of female lizards that court and attempt to copulate with other females—ultimately benefiting themselves by producing more eggs than females kept in isolation.

Veiled chameleon babies

In captivity, female veiled chameleons lay clutches of twenty to eighty eggs and sometimes store sperm for subsequent clutches. The brightly colored young, like the three pictured here, hatch after 168 to 220 days. The prehensile tails of baby veiled chameleons provide support by grasping branches of shrubs and eucalyptus trees on the high plateaus and forested mountain slopes of their native habitat.

Communication

"Reptiles, for the most part, are strangely silent," Schmidt and Inger once reflected. There are, of course, exceptions: crocodilians that bellow; snakes that hiss, rattle, or scrape their scales; and lizards that bark, grunt, squeak, click, chirp, hiss, cluck, or croak. The vocal lizards are primarily nocturnal geckos, but they are not the only species with communication skills. In fact, many lizards have developed elaborate repertoires of signals and displays for inter- and intraspecific communication, including chemical signals and visual displays involving color, posture, and movement.

Though perhaps not in the same league with the highly vocal frogs and toads, many geckos are adept at producing acoustic signals to attract mates, advertise territories, warn off intruders, and startle predators. The range of vocalizations embraces quite an array of sounds—and the name gecko is itself "onomatopoeic in origin," Bogert notes. *Geck-oh* or *to-kay* is the sound made by the large tokay gecko of Southeast Asia, famous for its loud call. The first-time visitor to Java and Malaysia, herpetologist Ulrich Gruber reports, often has the "startling experience of being awakened at night by a loud barking right next to his bed"—the sound of a tokay gecko that has taken up residence indoors.

"Many is the intimate scene . . . which *Gecko gecko* must have witnessed from its voyeur's lookout on the bungalow ceiling," Maurice Richardson surmises. He notes further that a family of loud-voiced tokays once inhabited a Malaysian billiard room and produced clicking sounds in response to the clicking of billiard balls.

Equally noisome is the barking gecko, a desert species from southern Africa that gathers in large choruses like frogs and calls early in the evening. Other renowned vocalists include the Madagascan day gecko, whose loud call Gruber compares to "the croaking of a tormented frog," and the flat-tailed gecko, which "sounds like a cat that has had its tail trodden on," Henkel and Schmidt relate. In addition to geckos—the only lizards that have vocal cords—certain other lizards can produce sounds too, including anoles, which may squeak when fighting or defending their territories; irritated iguanas, which may hiss when threatened; and Canary Islands lacertids, which vocalize during courtship.

Physical posturing and other visual displays by lizards are more familiar than their vocalizations. Many species—both in the wild and in captivity—display the same "stereotyped" or signature movements: bobbing the head, performing vigorous push-ups, inflating or compressing the body, lashing the tail, and extending the dewlap.

So many varieties of iguanids, from the small anoles to the large iguanas, display the characteristic head bobs and push-ups that scientists suspect the movements are ancestral traits. "The constancy of such a minor habit throughout most of the members of such a large family," Smith comments, is "striking." Among male anoles, head bobs usually signal an inclination to fight, reinforce territorial status, or engage in courtship. In conjunction with their rapid head movements, anoles also display their colorful dewlaps. "A green male courting amid green leaves can hardly be detected by the human observer," Greenberg and Noble report, "but the flash of a brilliant red is like a beacon light."

To test the hypothesis that bright hues play a role in species recognition, scientists have painted the dewlaps of anoles the colors of other species; when introduced, the altered males were attacked by aggressive resident males. Similarly, females that were equipped with an artificial dewlap were challenged or attacked by males of their own species.

A male anole that repeatedly flaunts its dewlap to attract a prospective mate or to warn an intruder can be quite theatrical. Authors Maurice and Robert Burton recall a spirited male anole in Barbados which, upon encountering its reflection in a mirror, immediately began flashing its dewlap. The first day, the anole put on a display for its perceived rival that lasted more than an hour; after that, it returned nearly every day. Sometimes it would peek behind the mirror, but its interest never waned; six weeks later, the anole was still making periodic treks to the mirror. I once placed a green anole in a terrarium that had a reflective metal strip at the base, and the startled male behaved in similar fashion. After forty-five minutes of vigorous head bobbing and dewlapping, however, it finally tired of its frantic efforts to attract the interest of the "intruder" and abandoned its quest.

Among the more ostentatious visual communicators are male frilled lizards of Australia, which erect large frills on each side of the neck, and male flying lizards of Asia, which extend their brilliantly colored "wings" to attract

Many chameleons communicate by altering their body size and changing color quickly, especially during the breeding season when males court females. Cryptic-colored species may expose gaudy colors and patterns to insure they become more conspicuous to the opposite sex. During aggressive interactions with other individuals, particularly between rival males, some chameleons flatten their bodies and turn sideways toward an intruder, or puff up their body to look larger and more threatening to rivals.

and excite females. Some lizards change color to catch a female's eye. Male five-lined and broadheaded skinks, for example, develop bright red or orange heads (or patches on their sides) during the breeding season. And the dramatic color changes of chameleons can signal an individual's current mood, including a sexually mature male's desire to attract a receptive female or to confront a rival male.

Certain species also communicate chemically by secreting a waxy substance from the femoral glands, located on the underside of the rear legs, or from cloacal or tail glands. Some skinks and desert iguanas, for example, apparently discriminate among species and between sexes by following chemical trails deposited on rocks and other substrate. Among certain Australian skinks, and perhaps other varieties, mothers can distinguish their own offspring by chemical cues. A flick of the tongue allows a lizard to investigate chemical stimuli by picking up particles and processing them with the Jacobson's organ. According to Pope, a teiid lizard (*Proctoporus shrevei*) found in caves on the island of Trinidad uses a very unusual form of visual communication: the tiny male produces or reflects a row of glowing lights along each side of its back, "suggesting to the observer portholes of a ship at night."

Anole flashing its dewlap
Male anoles extend their dewlap, or throat fan, to attract females, advertise their species and gender, and warn or challenge intruders and other males. This anole was photographed flashing its dewlap on the island of Bonaire, off the northern coast of Venezuela.

Defense Strategies

"The most common antipredator mechanism in lizards," herpetologists Daniel Cejudo and Rafael Márquez observe, "is fleeing." Such a defense strategy is sound indeed, especially for fleet-footed lizards such as racerunners and swifts. It is not, however, the only strategy. To insure their survival, lizards have evolved a variety of protective responses and tactics, from hiding, freezing, and fleeing to puffing up, hissing, gaping, snapping, biting, crying, charging, shedding their tail, squirting blood, and rolling into a ball by biting down on their tail or a limb.

Many lizards instinctively freeze when confronted by a predator, relying on cryptic or disruptive coloration and patterns for camouflage. Leafy greens and brown, tan, and gray earth tones offer protection to arboreal and terrestrial species; populations that colonize dark lava fields or light-colored sandy areas have evolved black or white "ground colors" that enhance their prospects for survival. Blotches, bands, stripes, and other patterns—known as "disruptive coloration"—conceal animals that freeze in place or dash off to a nearby hiding place. Researchers have determined that stripes on swift-moving reptiles (skinks and garter snakes, for example) "cause the eye to be deceived, making it difficult to keep the lizard in sight or to know which part of the body to attack," Mattison explains.

Lizards that escape to a crevice or burrow sometimes inflate their body, making it difficult for a predator to pry the lizard out of a narrow opening or to swallow it. In North America, the horned lizards, chuckwalla, crevice spiny lizard, and collared lizard are all accomplished body inflaters; a barrier of sharp spines on the tail offers additional protection once the animal is wedged into its rocky retreat.

Australia's frilled lizard responds to harassment by erecting an elaborate throat frill—sometimes characterized as the reptilian equivalent of Shakespeare's cowl—which startles attackers by suddenly enlarging the animal's size. (The flared ruff of the irritable, if fictional, dilophosaur in director Steven Spielberg's film *Jurassic Park* was modeled on that of the frilled lizard.) Bearded dragons also inflate their throat, projecting the long, pointed scales of their "beard" in a menacing fashion. These and other lizards will gape when threatened, displaying the bright colors of the lining of their mouth; blue-tongued skinks also waggle their bright tongues to startle predators.

Hissing is another common intimidation strategy, and some lizards squeak or issue a shrill cry. A horned lizard may hiss and lunge, or vibrate its tiny tail in dry leaves, creating an ominous rattling noise, authority Jane Manaster reports. The short but conspicuous spines and horns of horned lizards offer additional protection (snakes and other predators find them difficult to swallow), as do the claws, jaws, and armorlike bony plates of numerous other lizards.

Girdle-tailed lizards, also known as armadillo lizards and sungazers, defend themselves by grasping their tail, which is covered with sharp spines in rings or girdles, in their jaws. This creates a protective "stockade" around their vulnerable belly, Carr notes, as the body becomes a daunting hoop of plated scales. Similarly, the tiger or sandvelt lizard of Africa will grab a hind leg in its jaws to discourage predatory snakes, creating, in effect, a closed circle with no opening, Schmidt and Inger report. The savannah monitor rolls onto its back, assuming a similar defensive posture, and a few species simply feign death.

Three varieties of horned lizard employ a remarkable defense tactic that Manaster calls "the *coup de grace*": they squirt blood from sinuses in their eye sockets. By contracting muscles around the jugular vein, they raise the blood pressure in their head, Stebbins explains, which forces a "damming of blood and engorgement of the sinuses." The resulting thin stream of blood can spurt a distance of 4 feet (1.22 m), startling predators by irritating their eyes or producing a bad taste.

The venom of Gila monsters and beaded lizards is often assumed to be an offensive weapon, but it probably evolved as a defense mechanism—just as the bright pink-and-black or yellow-and-black beaded skin serves as an aposematic (warning-color) signal, Mattison suggests. Offensive too is the Gila monster's trick of defecating when handled, and Komodo dragons may defecate or vomit when preparing to fight. Three species of Australian geckos, Pianka reports, secrete a "smelly, noxious . . .

Lined leaf-tailed gecko
One of the most successful antipredator tactics of lizards is to avoid detection altogether by blending in with their natural surroundings. The coloration and stripe of this lined leaf-tailed gecko provide camouflage by making the lizard resemble a strip of brown tree bark.

sticky odoriferous goo" from external glands on their tail when disturbed. Equally effective is the juvenile Komodo dragon's penchant for rolling in fecal matter; since adults often cannibalize their youngsters, the scent of their own feces apparently provides a deterrent against consuming the flesh of fellow monitors.

One of the most celebrated of all lizard defense strategies is the discarding of the tail, a tactic known as autotomy. What would appear to be a painful act of self-mutilation is actually a well-evolved physiological process involving separation of vertebrae along a fracture plane; special muscles and organs in the lizard's tail minimize the loss of blood. While the wriggling tail continues to command the predator's attention, the lizard beats a hasty retreat. A new tail then grows at the site of the fracture, supported by cartilage rather than bone and slightly different in form and color.

Several varieties of Madagascan and South African geckos employ a defense mechanism called "shock-shedding" when handled by a human or grabbed by a predator. During shock-shedding, these lizards cast off large patches of skin at unique splitting zones. Shock-shedding appears not to injure the gecko, Henkel and Schmidt report, due to the "enormous powers of regeneration" of these species.

Short-horned lizard
The head and body of a short-horned lizard are covered with sharp spines that offer protection from snakes, birds, and other predators. In addition, some species of horned lizards are able to squirt blood from their eyes, which startles unsuspecting predators and repulses dogs, coyotes, and foxes.

Above:
Prehensile-tailed skink
The prehensile-tailed or Solomon Islands skink is a tree dweller equipped with strong limbs and sharp claws. When threatened, this giant skink will hiss menacingly at an intruder and sometimes inflict a painful bite. Adults are believed to offer protection to their young from boas, rats, and raptors.

Facing page:
Fence lizard
The brownish-gray coloration and crossbar patterns of a fence lizard provide camouflage on trees, logs, rail fences, and in dry, sandy woodlands. The fence lizard's spiny scales offer additional protection from predators.

Predation

Two modes of foraging predominate among the lizards, says Pianka: the "sit-and-wait" tactic and the "widely foraging" tactic. "Of course, this dichotomy is somewhat artificial," he continues, but "members of most lizard families typically exploit one or the other of these two modes. . . . Sit-and-wait predators rely largely on moving prey, whereas widely foraging predators encounter and consume nonmoving types of prey items more frequently." Pianka estimates that 60 percent of North American lizard species are sit-and-wait predators, while only 14 percent are foragers.

Employing one or the other tactic (or both), most lizards—especially smaller ones—are insectivores, stalking or lying in wait for bugs and other arthropods. A few lizards are herbivores, dining on plants, while others are omnivores, consuming both. The larger monitors are carnivores, eating small mammals, birds, and reptiles, and a few species are cannibals, devouring other lizards as well as their own offspring.

Among the best-known insectivores are skinks, geckos, and chameleons, although larger chameleons occasionally eat small birds and mammals. Geckos, which are celebrated for their ability to walk upside down on ceilings, stalk insects attracted to lights at night.

Some lizard species are "remarkably catholic in taste," Mattison says, and will eat "almost anything organic into which they can get their teeth," while others are dietary specialists. North American horned lizards and the Australian thorny devil, for example, eat primarily or exclusively ants (as many as 2,500 in a single meal), and several Australian and African lizards thrive on scorpions. The South American caiman lizard eats snails and mussels, using its flattened teeth to crush the shells, and the mountain stream lizard of China feeds on fish and tadpoles. Some nocturnal and diurnal skinks and at least one gecko are termite specialists; two New Zealand lizards enter water to catch mosquito larvae; and five-lined skinks have been observed shaking wasp nests and ambushing the emerging occupants.

To compensate for their leisurely gait, chameleons rely on their extraordinary tongue to ensnare insects and other prey at fantastic speeds. These "popgun tongues," Pope muses, "would be the horror of the African and Madagascan jungle if chameleons reached the dimensions of the larger crocodilians. Imagine walking through the forest, only to find yourself instantaneously transported to the open jaws of a perfectly camouflaged monster lurking some forty feet away."

Humans have good reason to be wary of Komodo dragons, which scavenge for carrion but also kill deer and goats. These huge monitors have been known to dig up islanders' bodies from shallow graves and to stalk and kill humans—ripping their flesh in surprise attacks or causing death by infection from deadly pathogens that thrive in their mouths.

In contrast to the flesh-loving Komodo dragon, the marine iguana dines exclusively on marine algae, which it finds on the seabed in cold ocean waters off the Galápagos Islands. On shore, Galápagos land iguanas—herbivores too—thrive on sharp-needled prickly pear cacti that grow on the arid islands. In Africa's Namib Desert, according to Pianka, one lacertid (*Aporosaura anchietae*) alternates sitting and waiting for airborne seeds when winds sweep across the desert with active foraging for insects when winds subdue.

Eastern bluebird with skink
Skinks and many other lizards are consumed by North American songbirds, wading birds, and birds of prey. Here, an Eastern bluebird is seen holding a small ground skink.

Hibernation

Lizards and other reptiles are ectotherms, which means they heat their bodies "from external sources, rather than generating their own body heat internally," herpetologist Richard Shine explains. One of the advantages for ectotherms is that they require "much less food," Shine says, "because they don't have to devote almost all of their energy into simply keeping warm," the way endotherms such as mammals and birds do. But because they are dependent on external heat, ectotherms must retreat below the frost line or seek other protection from freezing temperatures during cold weather.

For many species, Mertens explains, hibernation is essentially a "winter numbness," clearly caused by temperature, "whereas in others it is an inherited seasonal cycle." Lizards generally seek shelter in rocky crevices, tree trunks, burrows abandoned by other animals, beneath leaf litter, or in other protected sites. In some locations, lizards converge upon hibernacula (communal hibernation sites), such as the Iowa gravel pit where fifty-two skinks were once found massed together, or the rocky patch in Emporia, Kansas, where seven prairie skinks had buried themselves underground alongside twenty-one lined snakes.

"All temperate zone reptiles hibernate for several months in the year," Bellairs writes, "and species with a marginal distribution may hibernate in the colder but not in the warmer parts of their range." At higher altitudes, lizards also retreat when colder temperatures prevail.

In particularly dry surroundings, some lizards estivate (i.e., retreat to deep burrows and become dormant) to escape the intolerable heat and to avoid dehydration. While many herpetologists believe Gila monsters estivate, Bogert and del Campo suspect that these generally day-active animals change their habits and become nocturnal during warmer weather; as a result, they are less visible to casual observers.

Five-lined skink
Skinks throughout the United States and Canada hibernate when temperatures drop and adverse winter-weather conditions prevail. Some skinks hibernate beneath leaf litter, rocks, rotting logs, or a few inches of soil; others have been discovered at depths of 8 feet (2.44 m).

Lacerta

The lacertids of central and northern Europe, commonly known as wall lizards, select protected sites in which to hibernate during cold weather. One European herpetologist says lacertas allow themselves to be "supercooled," as they can withstand temperatures of 23.8° F (-4.75° C).

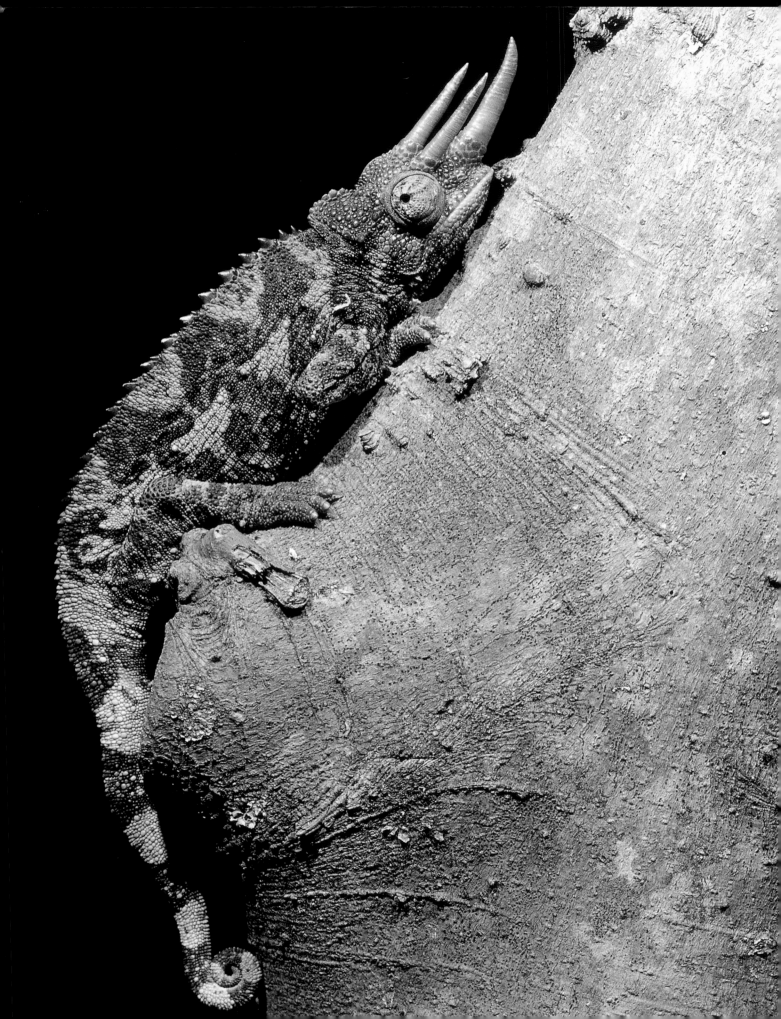

Chapter 3

Families and Species

Early taxonomists tended to lump all reptiles and amphibians together into one assembly of "foul and loathsome beasts," but today they generally divide them into two distinct classes: Amphibia and Reptilia. Traditionally, the living reptiles are classified into four major orders: (1) turtles, terrapins, and tortoises; (2) crocodilians; (3) tuataras (lizardlike animals from New Zealand); and (4) squamates (snakes, lizards, and amphisbaenians). This customary classification of snakes and lizards as "equal suborders" of Squamata "does not accurately reflect their interrelationships," Pough et al. argue. Nevertheless, "because of extensive differences in physiology, behavior, and functional morphology," lizards and snakes are usually treated separately.

Pough et al. recognize twenty-four families of lizards, and, as of December 2002, geneticist Peter Uetz and his associate T. Etzold had tallied 4,675 species of lizards for the European Molecular Biology Laboratory (EMBL) Reptile Database. (In comparison, they list only 2,940 species of snakes.) Not all herpetologists agree on these taxonomic classifications or species counts, however, and many a scientific battle has been fought over the "correct" assignment of names to families, genera, species, and subspecies.

Today, lizards are found on every continent, with the exception of the polar regions and some oceanic islands. In the Western Hemisphere, lizards inhabit a geographical range that extends from Canada to the tip of South America, and in the Eastern Hemisphere from southern Siberia, Finland, and Sweden southward through Australia and Africa. "Practically every Pacific island is provided with one or more species of lizards," Smith says, "derived from earlier direct connections with the continents or from accidental dispersal" by natural means or by human transport.

Some species inhabit a single island, while others are distributed across far-reaching stretches of geography. Whether living at high altitudes or low, near the Equator or far from it, lizards have demonstrated a remarkable ability to adapt, and, like their cousins the snakes, they inhabit a wide array of habitats, including tropical and temperate forests, mountains, deserts, swamps, grasslands, farmland, even suburbs and cities.

Jackson's chameleon
The male Jackson's chameleon sports three prominent horns or protuberances—two above the eyes and a third from the snout. These horns are sometimes used to joust with rival males during the breeding season, although individuals have been known to grasp their own horns when climbing and panic in their struggle to escape from themselves.

"Chameleons. Such exceptional creatures. The way they change color. Red. Yellow. Lime. Pink. Lavender. And did you know they are very fond of music?"

—*Truman Capote,* Music for Chameleons, *1980*

Like other reptiles, lizards occupy habitat niches that reflect preferences in climate, food supply, terrain, and vegetation. In the case of certain arboreal anoles, these niches may be as narrow as a specific zone or a single tree that supports different species at higher and lower portions of the tree. While some lizards are primarily burrowers, others are terrestrial, arboreal, or semiaquatic, and many shift easily between several such realms.

Jackson's Chameleon

Chamaeleo jacksonii

Visitors to Hawaiian locations used by film director Steven Spielberg in *Jurassic Park* may secretly yearn for a glimpse of a *T. rex* or other dinosaur species, yet if they look very carefully, they might just observe a miniature triceratops up in a tree. Actually, it's not a dinosaur, it's a Jackson's chameleon—a reptilian import sporting three giant horns (one on its snout and two above the eyes) and a helmet at the back of the head. No wonder tourists remark on the chameleon's resemblance to a triceratops.

In 1972, a Hawaiian pet-store owner released several dozen of these East African chameleons in his back yard, hoping the dehydrated animals might recover from the stress of overseas shipping; they escaped, slowly and methodically, and eventually established breeding colonies on the islands of Oahu, Maui, Hawaii, and Kauai. Scientists recognized at once why the exotic newcomers adapted so well to their new habitat: Hawaii offers high-altitude tropical forests and heavy rainfall similar to those of the lizards' native Kenya, Tanzania, Uganda, and Mozambique.

Males of the species bear the three trademark horns (two pointing forwards and the third slightly upward), while females have only three small lumps or a single nubby spike. The function of the horns is subject to some debate. Some authorities believe the giant spikes on males serve primarily to attract females and to deter enemies. Others report males wield their horns to joust with rivals and knock them off perches.

The color of Jackson's chameleon varies among the three subspecies (called, with some affection, "the Jacksons"). When resting, most individuals are a shade of green—bright green, lime green, olive green, or yellow green—but the colors and patterns change swiftly to brown or black (or a medley of colors) and expose bands or irregular flecks when the lizard is stimulated or stressed. Many look drab in the morning, when darker colors absorb sunlight and warm the lizard more rapidly than lighter hues. During much of the day, however, these chameleons are especially difficult to distinguish from lichen prevalent on the trees these creatures favor. Young Jacksons are usually tan or light gray.

Besides their distinctive horns and helmet, the Jacksons also have a crest running down their back with a row of toothlike spines. Their remarkably versatile eyes project from cone-shaped turrets and operate independently of each other; their fused toes create four practical sets of pincers; and their prehensile tail, used for gripping and balancing, conveniently rolls up when not in use. The celebrated tongue, roughly one and a half times the lizard's length, shoots out and snatches prey in a mere fraction of a second.

Like many other lizards, the Jackson's chameleon has its own special mating ritual. When two rival males meet, the highly territorial animals stage a dramatic showdown: they turn sideways, puff up their body to appear more imposing, and then curl their tail. Typically, their skin colors brighten as they thrust their head forward, sway and bob, and raise up their front legs. Some males open their mouth to flaunt the bright inner colors and hiss. Then the clash of horns begins.

If an opponent is physically injured during a joust or decides to retreat, the victorious male will turn his medley of threat displays toward an available female; if she is not ready to mate, she responds with her own threatening gestures. (Weak or no gestures signal her apparent willingness to mate.) The male then circles around the female, bites her neck, and inserts one hemipenis. Approximately 190 days later, the ovoviviparous female gives birth to as many as forty living young, each bursting through a sticky, glasslike amniotic sac on the branch where it has been deposited. Newborns, as well as adults, eat insects, caterpillars, slugs, snails, and earthworms. When fully grown, individuals attain lengths of 10 to 13¾ inches (25 to 35 cm).

The Jackson's chameleon, observes authority Carl Reyes, is "far from an intelligent species—'slow' not only in its movements but also in thinking. They have been known to grab their own horn while climbing, resulting in a panicked struggle as the animal tries to escape from itself."

Jackson's chameleon

The Jackson's chameleon resembles a miniature triceratops. These arboreal chameleons inhabit East Africa's cool highland forests and mountain thickets, where their cryptic green to yellow-brown coloration and patterns offer protection in bright foliage and on lichen-covered tree bark.

Panther Chameleon

Furcifer pardalis

Along the northern and eastern coasts of Madagascar, and on neighboring islands, lives a gaudy, aggressive creature that hisses, gapes, turns an angry red, eats its own offspring, and engages in fights to the finish. Fortunately, this creature has no quarrel with humans and poses no threat, even though superstitious islanders believe it to be poisonous.

This animal is neither a venomous serpent nor a deranged lemur—it's the panther chameleon, so named because of its aggressive nature. The panther is surely one of the world's most spectacular chameleons. When not provoked, males are a luminous lime green or dark green, with a pale blue stripe running along each side from the back of the head to the hind leg. Numerous dark green or rust-colored crossbands are visible, along with a generous stippling of orange, white, and other brightly colored scales. When threatened by a rival male or female, brilliant reds and yellows and splashes of other colors abruptly supplant the greens, Martin reports. Females, ordinarily gray brown, advertise their availability for mating by first turning salmon orange and then darkening to black with orange markings.

Panther chameleons vary in color not only between individuals and sexes but from one locale to the next. Widely distributed throughout Madagascar's humid rain forests, these fascinating creatures are now also found near human populations—along weedy roadsides, in farmers' fields, even in garden trees.

Panther chameleon
One of the world's most spectacularly colored chameleons, the panther chameleon of Madagascar sports variable shades of green and turquoise blue, highlighted with vivid splashes of red, salmon, orange, yellow, and brown.

Panther chameleon
Panther chameleons are an object of superstition in Madagascar. Some islanders avoid touching these lizards, and drivers will even swerve suddenly just to avoid hitting one as it ambles slowly across a roadway.

Male panthers may grow as long as 21½ inches (55 cm), including the tail, and are notoriously territorial, challenging rivals by inflating their body, gaping, butting heads, and lunging. According to Martin, the first to charge will usually prevail, and the intimidated opponent will flee or drop to the ground. "But if fighting ensues, one will grab the other and bite fiercely, tearing the flesh and crushing bones . . . leaving the weakened animal to face a slow death."

"Panther romance," Martin continues, "displays similar savagery." Sighting a female in his territory, a male will give chase, twitching and bobbing his head frantically before he seizes and mounts her. Soon after mating, the female descends to the sand and digs a burrow in broad daylight, where she lays a clutch of thirty to fifty eggs. Afterwards, she fills in the burrow with dirt, taps it down to hide the entrance to the burrow, and lumbers off. Instead of hatching simultaneously, the babies emerge over the course of several months. About eight months later (this time may vary depending upon humidity and altitude) the hatchlings begin to emerge, "ready to fight," Martin adds, with "all weapons systems operating at 100% efficiency."

Superstitions about these lizards cause native Madagascans to both fear the chameleons (women are forbidden to handle them, and men who do cannot touch their wives for three days) and protect them (killing a panther is said to bring bad luck). "Taxi drivers who think nothing of hitting a chicken or a dog swerve wildly to avoid a panther," Martin notes, and traffic sometimes grinds to a halt while motorists wait for a slow-moving panther to shuffle across the road.

Flap-Necked Chameleon

Chamaeleo dilepis

Because of its widespread distribution throughout central and southern Africa, the flap-necked chameleon is often referred to as the "common chameleon," much to the confusion of people who know Europe's *Chamaeleo chamaeleon* by the same name. But the African species is recognized by flaps on either side of its head, which it raises and wiggles when excited. Pet owners report this occurs fairly often, as it appears that flap-necked chameleons are nervous and easily stressed. Males generally live alone and guard their territory "jealously," according to Martin, and they can be quite aggressive, challenging intruders with "vigorous countermeasures."

In addition to wiggling their flaps (individually or simultaneously), these green, tan, or brown chameleons display bright yellow and orange colors on the interstitial skin of their throat pouch. If a flap-necked chameleon should encounter a boomslang (a highly venomous, and extremely swift, arboreal serpent), the lizard will flash its brightly colored dewlap, puff up its body, and hiss. "But the snake, as a rule, is little impressed by this and refuses to be deterred," states Herbert Schifter. If the intruder is a human, however, the lizard may deliver a painful bite to discourage handling.

Flap-necked chameleons grow to a maximum length of about 15 inches (38 cm), including tail, and feed on a variety of insects. In dry forest and savannah habitats, females descend to the ground and dig tunnels in which they deposit as many as fifty-eight eggs.

Flap-necked chameleon
The flap-necked chameleon, with a range that extends through tropical and southern Africa, is named for the pair of flaps located behind the male's helmet. The male holds these flaps erect and wiggles them when he confronts another chameleon.

Mountain Chameleon

Chamaeleo (Trioceros) montium

Inhabiting the humid montane cloud forests of Cameroon is a spectacularly colored chameleon known by many names, including the mountain, mountain horned, mountain two-horned, and Cameroon sailfin chameleon. Tourists to western Africa marvel at the lizard's vivid colors, which resemble the bright hues of new leaves. When not feeling stressed, males are "clad in scales of lime green (at times bordering on chartreuse) with highlights of yellow, turquoise, robin's-egg blue, and terra-cotta or peach," note R. D. and Patricia Bartlett.

Mertens once observed a particularly resplendent mountain chameleon that was challenging several rival males; its leaf-green skin began to exhibit colors of "rare beauty," including sky-blue spots and glowing yellow and coal-black dots. Meanwhile, its rivals turned a dark shade of greenish black, but displayed no markings at all. In contrast, females often have streaks of red on their green bodies.

On the tip of its snout, each male has two long ringed horns, which differ in size and shape. During the breeding season, males wield these curved, forward-pointing horns in territorial battles with other males. (Females lack horns and sport small conelike vestiges instead.) Males also have a low ribbed keel or crest known as a "sailfin" that extends down the back and partway down the tail.

Adult mountain chameleons, represented by three or four subspecies, range from 6 to 12 inches in total length (15 to 30.5 cm). Their habitat comprises cool, high-altitude mountain forests where seasonal rainfall is plentiful and sunlight is restricted by cloud cover. Generally found on trees, shrubs, and elephant grass during the day, these lizards sleep on branches at night with their head lowered and tail coiled tightly. When they feel threatened, Manfred Rogner says, these chameleons drop from their perch and "flee very quickly"—for a chameleon—"or lie still on the ground." Mountain chameleons also dig holes in the ground as protective retreats.

Females deposit clutches of five to sixteen large eggs in the moist substrate. Hatchlings as well as adults thrive on insects and mealworms.

Mountain chameleon

A pair of horns on the male's head and a sailfin crest running down the back and part of the tail are distinguishing characteristics of the West African mountain chameleon. When feeling stressed, these beautiful bright-green lizards turn drab shades of brown or olive and sometimes drop to the ground from their perch in a tree and pretend to be dead.

Green Anole

Anolis carolinensis

In *Music for Chameleons*, New Orleans–born author Truman Capote claims he once watched three "green chameleons" race one another across a stately terrace and pause at his hostess' feet. "Chameleons [are] such exceptional creatures," remarked the hostess. "Did you know they are very fond of music?" Capote was skeptical, so his friend sat down at her piano and began playing a Mozart sonata.

"Eventually the chameleons accumulated," Capote recalled; "a dozen, a dozen more, most of them green. . . . They skittered across the terrace and scampered into the salon, a sensitive, absorbed audience for the music." Afterwards, when the pianist rose from her bench, "the chameleons scattered like sparks from an exploding star."

How charmingly exotic—but do chameleons really respond to music? In truth, Capote was observing anoles, which many Americans persist in calling "chameleons" because of their similar talent for changing color. But Capote, one suspects, would not have been pleased with the less elegant-sounding title *Music for Anoles*.

However you pronounce the name ("uh-NO-lee," "AN-ole," or "uh-nole"), this lizard is an exceptional creature. Scientists recognize more than 350 species worldwide, the largest genus of any lizard, and green anoles of the Southern United States are especially popular as pets. A century ago, fashionable women even attached them by threads to their dresses as a sort of "living jewelry."

Herpetologist Eric Pianka recalls his first encounter with a green anole at the age of six. "Somewhere in the South," he remembers, his family stopped "at a roadside park for a picnic lunch. There I saw my first lizard, a gorgeous, green, sleek, long-tailed arboreal creature. . . . We did our utmost to capture that lizard, but all we were able to get was its tail. I still remember standing there holding its twitching tail, wishing intensely that it was the lizard instead."

Unlike most other lizards, the green anole allows humans to approach closely, trusting its cryptic colors (green and brown) to provide camouflage. Growing roughly 5 to 8 inches (12.5 to 20.3 cm) long, including the tail, and ranging from North Carolina south to Key West and westward to the Rio Grande Valley, green anoles spend most of their time in shrubs, vines, and trees; they are often found on fences or walls near gardens, searching for insects. These anoles will climb high at night to sleep, and Carr recalls watching many fall 40 or 50 feet from trees in his Florida yard without suffering any apparent damage.

Robust, light on their feet, and excellent climbers (their toe pads enable them to climb vertical surfaces, including glass), green anoles have expressive eyes, a long snout, and a slender, streamlined body ("like a miniature alligator," quips one naturalist, "or a dachshund without ears"). These anoles can be nearly as contentious as alligators (or dachshunds): when two males confront one another, they circle warily, puff out their throats, threaten with open jaws, and rush to bite. After their jaws interlock, note Schmidt and Inger, the lizards shake their heads vigorously "until one or both fall from the branch."

Green anoles are famous for their fanfare: they bob their head and perform ritualistic push-ups with style, but when they spread their red (or pink) dewlap like an Oriental fan, the sudden flare truly commands attention. Males display their brightly colored dewlap when they spot a female or wish to challenge a rival male.

In other *Anolis* species, dewlap colors range from red, orange, yellow, and white to blue and purple, and they are "important for species recognition," Pough et al. explain. "While the advertisement or assertion displays of territorial male lizards elicit aggressive responses from other males or cause them to retreat, these same displays are attractive to females."

Of course, it is the green anole's talent for rapid color change that makes it so irresistible. Contrary to popular belief, the color of the lizard's background does not prompt the change; rather, it is such factors as light, temperature, mood, excitement level, and physical activity. Anoles exposed to direct sunlight, for example, will turn emerald green, but when the sun disappears or the temperature drops, they turn dark brown. If frightened or confronting a rival, anoles turn bright green, and when sleeping at night their skin customarily remains green.

Internally, the release of a hormone by the pituitary gland causes changes in the concentrations of pigments, resulting in the transformation from green to brown or vice versa. An intermediate shade of gray is sometimes visible, and blue specimens occasionally appear due to a lack of yellow pigments.

During the mating season, amorous males approach females, which, if receptive, "turn the head to one side in a gesture we can only describe as coy," Schmidt and Inger declare. When the female points her snout downward, the male clasps her neck in his jaws, intertwines his tail around hers, and they copulate. Females deposit either a single egg or a pair of eggs at eight-day intervals throughout the summer, usually in rotting wood or leaf litter. On occasion, females have been observed pushing an egg with their snout, or even rolling it some distance, in search of a more suitable location.

Green anole on bromeliad
North America's misnamed "chameleon" is actually the green anole, a slender tree- and fence-climbing lizard with leaf-green coloration that can change suddenly, depending on the temperature and other stimuli. Males extend their pinkish-red dewlap, which is attached to the throat, during courtship and when challenging intruders.

Jamaican Giant Anole

Anolis garmani

Jamaican giant anoles, also called crown supergiant anoles, are "the true giants of the anole world . . . the kings of their realm," researchers at the Caribbean Anole Database declare. Their realm, it turns out, is not limited to Jamaica and neighboring Caribbean islands: these lizards are also firmly ensconced in Miami and southern Florida and hold the title of America's largest introduced anole species. Jamaican giant anoles were first found in the wild in Florida in the mid-1980s—probably escapees from pet dealers or importers.

Growing to a maximum length of nearly 12 inches (30.5 cm), including tail, the Jamaican giant anole is typically bright leaf-green in color, turning dark brown at night. Some males have straw-colored crossbands, and females may have spots; hatchlings and juveniles are generally paler than adults. The male has a large yellow or white dewlap, usually with an orange center, and the female has a smaller, darker throat fan.

Males can be recognized by their massive casque-shaped head and prominent crest of enlarged scales on their neck and back. According to the Caribbean Anole Database, these lizards also have a "powerful tail, very powerful jaws, and a mean temperament."

Jamaican giant anoles generally live in pairs in the canopy of trees; together, the male and female vigorously defend their territory, which may comprise several trees. The Bartletts have found these anoles to be "more complacent" about allowing humans to approach them than are many smaller anole species. Jamaican giants on shade trees "would allow us to get within 2 ft (61 cm) of them," the Bartletts note. "Any nearer than this and the lizards would tense, then dart away with a speed and agility unexpected from such a large creature."

During extremely warm weather, Jamaican giant anoles spend more time close to the ground, perched on the trunk of a tree with their snout pointed downward. When they spot approaching prey—chiefly insects, other arthropods, and occasionally birds, small mammals, or other anoles—these lizards leap from the tree to snatch their meal, then return to the treeside perch to swallow it. Jamaican giants sometimes eat fruit, including Virginia creeper berries and other foliage. After mating, females lay clutches of one or two soft-shelled oval eggs in loose substrate or in decomposing plant matter, often in the fork of a tree.

Jamaican giant anole

Called the "kings of their realm," Jamaican giant anoles live in pairs in a tree canopy, which they defend fiercely. Both sexes are a vivid leaf-green color, except at night when they turn brown; males have a prominent serrated crest down the back, and their dewlap is lemon yellow with an orange center.

Madagascan Giant Day Gecko

Phelsuma madagascariensis grandis

Madagascar's day geckos are often called "living jewels," and it's obvious why: while most of the world's geckos are nocturnal and cryptic in color, these geckos are diurnal (day-active) and boast stunning neon-bright skin of emerald green (or turquoise or deep forest green), garnished with red stripes on the head and bright splashes of red or "dayglo orange" on the neck and body. Patches of blue may be visible too. The intensity of the hues varies dramatically, Ken Preston-Mafham writes in *Madagascar: A Natural History*; in some forested areas, giant day geckos are "disappointingly dull," while they are "far more beautiful" and "dazzlingly sumptuous" in other areas.

A native of northern Madagascar and neighboring Nosy Be ("Big Island"), the giant day gecko really *is* a giant (at least for a day gecko), growing to almost 12 inches (30.5 cm). These lizards are arboreal, commonly found on banana plants, palms, and other trees. In villages, they perch conspicuously on the trunks of shade trees, on walls, and on roofs.

The day gecko's provocatively flamboyant coloration probably evolved to catch the eye of prospective mates (and to signal rivals), although Preston-Mafham says it is a mystery "how such a conspicuous creature, presenting such an apparently easy target for every predator in the vicinity, manages to avoid being picked off." Conceivably, the neon-green ground color harmonizes with the shimmer of leaves of tropical vegetation, and the disruptive streaks of red and orange resemble the bright blossoms of native flowers.

Unlike so many of their gecko cousins, Madagascan giant day geckos hang onto the trunks of trees or other objects with their head facing upward rather than downward; if disturbed, they simply loosen their grip and fall from their perch, using their tail for balance, and land on their feet like a cat. Because their skin tears easily when grasped, these geckos often startle predators and slip away.

When a male courts a female, he bobs his head energetically and waves his tail, much as he would threaten a rival male, Henkel and Schmidt report, noting, "Whether bites are inflicted depends largely on the behaviour of the female." One breeder chanced to observe the courtship of a pair in captivity: the male approached the female, flicked his tongue rapidly, and both lizards vocalized a low, raspy *keck* sound. The male then grabbed the female by the neck, maneuvered his lower body around her, anchored her against the wall, and inserted his hemipenis.

Females customarily lay two eggs—called a "double clutch"—which stick to each other. The female lies on her back to lay the first egg, rotating it "until it is almost spherical," Henkel and Schmidt write. After laying a second egg and rotating it like the first, she presses the two together until they stick; when the shells have hardened, the female affixes them to a leaf or moves them to a protected hiding place.

Madagascan giant day geckos are sit-and-wait predators that consume a variety of small insects. Specimens available from pet dealers have been bred in captivity, since all Madagascan day geckos are protected and their trade restricted.

Madagascan giant day gecko
Now bred widely by herpetoculturists outside Madagascar, the giant day gecko is emerald green with variable flecks of red. Partial to palms and banana trees and the walls of village houses, Madagascan giant day geckos have keen eyesight and are able escape their enemies with quick bursts of speed.

Crested, or eyelash, gecko

A crest of scales resembling eyelashes that runs from above the eye to the shoulder gives this gecko from New Caledonia its name. These "eyelashes" may protect the eyes when the gecko burrows into loose soil or leaf litter with its pointed snout, or they may serve as sensory devices.

Crested Gecko

Rhacodactylus ciliatus

The family history of the New Caledonian crested gecko is an interesting, if cautionary, one: for a long time this lizard was considered extinct. Although originally discovered in 1866, this curious-looking gecko from the French island territory of New Caledonia, roughly 1,000 miles (1,600 km) east of Australia, was not seen again in the wild for so many years that collectors concluded the species had become extinct.

But after a tropical storm in 1994, a single specimen was found on the Isle of Pines. Field trips by Wilhelm Henkel and Philippe de Vosjoli revealed widespread distribution of the species on the Isle of Pines, and additional specimens turned up on Grande Terre and Koutomo islands. Today, as a result of successful captive-breeding programs, crested geckos are widely available in the pet trade, and smuggling of wild-caught specimens appears to have decreased significantly.

The rediscovery of the crested gecko—also known as the eyelash gecko, though no relation to Australia's eyelash gecko (*Diplodactylus ciliaris*)—delighted conservationists and reptile enthusiasts alike, in part because of the species' peculiar physical characteristics. A dozen or more pointy "eyelash" scales project over each eye, and a row of similarly pointed scales or "temporal crests" extends from behind each eye and along the shoulder.

These "eyelashes" are not mere decoration, however—they serve a useful purpose. Although this semi-arboreal gecko spends its nights in trees, wrapping its prehensile tail around branches for a secure grip, it digs burrows in loose soil or leaf litter to hide by day. When the crested gecko plows its shovel-like snout into the substrate, pressure exerted on the eyelash scales causes the eyeballs to recess and the upper eyelid to partially cover the eye, explain de Vosjoli and Frank Fast.

If disturbed on the ground during the day, the crested gecko will assume a typical defensive stance—raising up its body on all four legs to look as large as possible, opening its jaws, and gaping threateningly. If startled while in a tree at night, the lizard will "drop to the ground, curl snout to tail and lie still," note de Vosjoli and Fast, who hypothesize that lying motionless may protect the lizard from owls, which have excellent hearing and share the primary-forest habitat with these geckos.

New Caledonian crested geckos display a variety of colors—including yellow, orange, red, brown, tan, and rust—and reportedly become brighter and lighter at night. They grow to a maximum length of about 8 inches (20 cm), including the tail, but adult lizards in the wild seldom possess more than just the stub of their original tail. "In adults, tails can literally be a drag," de Vosjoli and Fast write, "and seem to get in the way of easy locomotion and jumping." Curiously, their tails do not grow back, except for the nub at the base.

Crested geckos are more social than most lizards and do not exhibit signs of territorial aggressiveness. In captivity, females can be kept in "harems" (several females to each male); after mating, they lay clutches of two eggs at one-month intervals—up to twenty eggs per year. In their native habitat, crested geckos are primarily herbivorous, feeding on a variety of fruits; in captivity, they thrive on bananas and small insects.

Leopard Gecko

Eublepharis macularius

Typically sporting a yellow or sandy-hued ground color, the leopard gecko owes its name to its prominent black or brownish-black spots. These "leopard spots" emerge as the gecko grows older, since most juveniles are born with chocolate-brown bands that fade gradually into small spots or flecks. In recent years, this species has become enormously popular with hobbyists; today, selectively bred "designer" leopard geckos are identified as jungle, ghost, diamondback, tangerine, Halloween, or other strains.

Leopard geckos are natives of Asia and the Middle East, where they inhabit arid and semi-arid rocky deserts and grasslands and mountain habitats at elevations up to 7,000 feet (2.1 km). During the day, leopard geckos take refuge under rocks or in holes; at dusk, they emerge to stalk insect prey, moving in serpentine fashion and often wriggling their tail like a cat. With their distinctive turnip-shaped tails (which store fat), tubercled scales, and moveable eyelids (which permit them to close their eyes), these geckos are easy to recognize. Small claws assist in climbing, since the lamellae on their toes do not cling to surfaces.

Males are highly territorial and do not tolerate the presence of other males. Females lay pairs of eggs as often as ten times during the breeding season; prior to laying, the eggs are visible through the translucent skin of a gravid female's belly. Scientists have discovered that the incubation temperature of leopard gecko eggs determines the sex of the hatchlings: 79° to 80° F (approximately 26° C) will produce mostly females, while temperatures from 90° to 92° F (approximately 32° to 33° C) will produce males.

Leopard gecko

Equipped with a pair of movable eyelids, the leopard gecko of Afghanistan, Iraq, and Iran can actually close its eyes and, in the opinion of some pet owners, wink. This nocturnal lizard has a yellow ground color with dark "leopard" spots, although juveniles sport prominent contrasting bands of yellow and chocolate brown that fade with age.

Fat-tailed gecko

The prominent tail of the African fat-tailed gecko stores fat, but the appendage is often cast off when the gecko seeks to escape a predator. The skin has a velvety appearance, and the morph, or interbreeding population, of this individual has a white stripe that runs down the back from the head to the tip of the tail.

Fat-Tailed Gecko

Hemitheconyx caudicinctus

Like the leopard gecko, the fat-tailed gecko has a bulbous, turnip-shaped tail that stores fat. But the tip of the tail is rounded rather than pointed, and this gecko also has a rounder snout and shorter toes with weaker claws. And while the leopard gecko's bands turn to spots as the lizard matures, adult fat-tailed geckos retain their vivid chocolate-brown bands. Some individuals also sport a white stripe down their back, from the head to tip of the tail.

A native of West Africa, this species ranges from Senegal to northern Cameroon, where it inhabits dry open woodlands, savannahs, and rocky hillside slopes. Averaging 8 to 10 inches (20.3 to 25.4 cm) in length, this lizard has a hunting strategy the Bartletts characterize as "both interesting and, at times, comical." The fat-tailed gecko's approach to its prey—chiefly insects and other arthropods—"may be either stealthy or darting, and is often accompanied by an accentuated amount of tail-writhing and posturing," the Bartletts say.

Males have larger heads and more powerful bodies than females and are highly territorial. According to Rogner, males try to catch a female "unawares," inflicting a "firm bite" on the neck to grip them while mating. Females bury pairs of soft-shelled eggs throughout the breeding season, and incubation temperatures determine the sex of the offspring. Like leopard geckos, fat-tails have moveable eyelids and, the Bartletts suggest, "seem to wear perpetually bemused smiles."

Namib Desert Gecko

Palmatogecko rangei

"Swimming" across the desert sands of coastal southwestern Africa, the Namib Desert gecko has webbed feet with thin, pliable membranes between its toes that allow it to skim over loose sand like snowshoes, says Mattison. This small gecko, only about 4½ to 5½ inches (11 to 14 cm) in total length, has very slender, almost fragile limbs and a soft, velvety skin so transparent that its internal organs shimmer through and create what some observers describe as a "ghostly" appearance.

Contributing to the otherworldly look of this lizard are its enormous eyes, which bulge like a movie alien's and accentuate the dark red irises and vertical pupils. To a nocturnal gecko, oversized eyes are invaluable for catching prey in the dark; during the day, however, this species retreats into tunnels it digs in the dunes. Interestingly, the Namib Desert provides its own source of moisture: cold ocean currents cause dense fogs, which roll in from the coast and periodically enshroud the desert. Geckos obtain moisture from these mists and the resulting dew.

The Namib Desert cools off quickly at night, but these geckos tolerate temperatures as low as 50° F (10° C) and actively dart about in search of prey—termites, beetles, sand crickets, and other insects. Residents of the area, according to visitor Rick Staub, have an apropos saying: "This night is so cold it is only fit for a palmatogecko."

Males of the species produce squeaks and clicks during territorial disputes with other males, and they approach females "stealthily" during the breeding season, according to Rogner, before springing toward them and seizing them by the neck. Later, the females will bury their sticky eggs in loose soil, but only after rolling them in dry sand "until they are completely covered in a protective coat," which hardens in a few minutes, Rogner explains.

Namib Desert gecko
Active by night, the Namib Desert gecko digs tunnels in the sandy dunes of southern Africa's Namib Desert to retreat from the daytime heat. The thin, nearly transparent skin is pinkish brown with dark bands. Webbing on its feet permits this lizard to skim across the desert sands as if wearing snowshoes.

Five-Lined Skink

Eumeces fasciatus

Escorpión—or the "scorpion lizard"—is a rather alarming name for a lizard. But, Carr reports, "all the way from North Carolina to Panama, people unversed in herpetology call one skink or another 'scorpion' and consider them to be venomous." Prominent among them is the five-lined skink, earmarked as a suspect because of its conspicuously bright blue tail. Coral snakes, monarch butterflies, and other animals have evolved aposematic (warning) colors to advertise their toxicity. Thus, Carr points out, the blue tail "looks for all the world like a sign that the bearer is either venomous or toxic." But Carr confirms skinks are neither, although he says some Florida pet owners blame skinks when their pets suffer gastric illnesses or paralysis.

There are, in fact, several possible explanations why the tails of five-lined skinks are so bright. Juveniles and adult females may have evolved their electric-blue tails as a distraction: a predator might be more likely to attack the disposable tail than the head, enhancing the odds that the lizard would live to see another day. When the tail snaps off—the result of an escape reflex called autotomy—the severed appendage continues to vibrate and jerk, covering the skink's retreat.

Another hypothesis is that bright tails are used as lures to attract small prey. Many foraging skinks, Carr points out, routinely wave their tails. But the blue tail and, for that matter, the five white or yellowish stripes that give this skink its name do not last into old age. As the skink matures, the blue gradually disappears or fades to gray, the stripes darken, and the black or dark-brown ground color lightens to dull olive. Adult males acquire an orange-red head during the breeding season and eventually lose their stripes altogether.

The scales of the five-lined skink are especially distinctive. Ditmars describes them as "smooth, shining, almost glassy"; other observers characterize them as glossy, highly polished, wet, or varnished-looking, with the sheen of enamel. The five-lined skink can grow to about 8½ inches (21.6cm) in length, including the tail—which, herpetologists note, seldom appears in its entirety, due to its proclivity to break off.

Because of its extensive range, which stretches from Massachusetts to northern Florida and west to Texas, Oklahoma, Kansas, and Wisconsin, this skink is one of America's best-known lizards. In upper New England, in fact, it is the *only* native lizard found in the wild.

This lizard prefers habitats that provide shelter beneath leaves, debris, rotting wood, rocks, and other surface objects, such as deciduous and evergreen forests, the margins of woods and fields, and cleared lots with rotting logs and stumps. Five-lined skinks are celebrated for their wariness: herpetologists routinely remark how difficult they are to catch, darting off in a flash at the glimpse of any human who moves in their direction. If somehow caught, they employ one last line of defense: nipping their captor with their tiny jaws.

Though primarily terrestrial and fond of basking on logs or rockpiles, five-lined skinks will dart up a tree or bush if threatened. Observers often glimpse them near trash heaps and Dumpsters—not because the garbage itself is alluring, but because it attracts flies and other insects that skinks eat.

According to authority Henry Fitch, five-lined skinks are not territorial, although some males are belligerent toward other males during the breeding season. Courting consists of "rushing with open mouth at the neck of any lizard of the species that may be around," Smith says; "if the object of the rush fights back, it is identified as a male by the courting animal, which turns its attention to others." Fights can be violent and produce serious injury, although the defeated male usually hides to evade his opponent.

When a male encounters a skink that puts up no resistance, "such lizards are identified as females," Smith notes, "and mating ensues." The male grasps a receptive female by her neck and holds her in his jaws while wrapping his tail around hers and slipping his cloaca into position beneath hers. Copulation is brief, although over time a female may mate with several males.

After laying a clutch of up to eighteen eggs, the female engages in a behavior rare for any reptile: she remains with her eggs. Although she curls her body around the clutch, the female apparently does not "incubate" them; instead, she protects them from harm. Females periodically roll or turn their eggs, apparently to insure adequate moisture or prevent rotting, and will even empty their bladder on the substrate to keep them moist. Occasionally, a female emerges to drink, bask, or feed, according to Fitch, but she often "satisfies her hunger by devouring one of her own eggs."

Several females may be found protecting their eggs in the same rotting log or burrow, and these skinks sometimes overwinter together in communal hibernation sites. Researchers have discovered that five-lined skinks can discriminate among the pheromones left by other lizards. Adults, says Tyning, "are usually attracted to odors given off by other members of the same species and thus follow a trail to them or attempt to get closer."

Five-lined skink
One of the most widely distributed lizards in North America, the five-lined skink has shiny, polished scales; yellow or bluish-white stripes on a black, brown, or other dark ground color; and a vivid blue tail that fades with age. Although commonly seen basking on logs and leaves, these skinks are quite skittish and dart for cover when disturbed.

Prehensile-Tailed Skink

Corucia zebrata

The prehensile-tailed skink, a secretive species found in tropical forests of the Solomon Islands, has the distinction of being the world's largest skink. With a tail even longer than its body, this lizard (also called the giant skink or Solomon Islands skink) can attain a total length of around 30 inches (76 cm), although measuring the tail of a preserved specimen can be difficult, Pope observes, because "it becomes curled and brittle."

This arboreal species is the only skink with a prehensile tail, which, like a monkey's or chameleon's tail, can grasp branches and provide stability. This skink has a broad head; a short, blunt snout; large ear openings; and very large scales that are exceptionally smooth and shiny.

The species name, *zebrata*, refers to the lizard's dark-brown zebralike stripes or bars that cross a pale-olive or greenish-white back. Rogner describes these skinks as "normally quite peaceful animals," but when threatened they may hiss loudly, charge an intruder, and inflict a painful bite. During the day they can be seen sleeping alone on branches (fig trees are favored) or in groups in cavities of trees, descending after dark to eat fallen fruit or the leaves of climbing vines.

Females are ovoviviparous and produce just one or two offspring at ten- or twelve-month intervals. Curiously, the babies often remain with their parents, Rogner reports, which defend them against predators such as Solomon Island boas, rats, shrews, and raptors.

Prehensile-tailed skink
The Solomon Islands are the home of this whopper, the world's largest skink. The prehensile-tailed skink leads a secretive lifestyle in coastal forests, where its strong tail muscles provide a secure grip and permit the lizard to hang from the branches of fig trees.

Gila Monster

Heloderma suspectum

"I've seed a lizzard what could outpizen any frog or toad in the world," an anonymous blowhard boasted in the San Diego *World* in 1873. "[I] went after it with a stick, but the thunderin' thing, instead of runnin' away like any nateral lizard, squatted on its tail and spit at me. . . . I got so mad I shook the pistol in the critter's face, and I'm a liar if it didn't jump at it and ketch the muzzle in its mouth. . . . I believe Mister Lizzard would hev pulled me plum into the river if I hadn't thought to shoot down his throat."

Mister Lizzard was, of course, a Gila monster, a venomous creature vilified over the years as "ugly," "repulsive," "a walking septic tank," and "the Boris Karloff of the desert." Yet it may also be, as Smith once put it, "the most extraordinary lizard of the country."

Probably named after the Gila River in Arizona, where it was once abundant, this creature was styled a "monster" because it and the other member of its genus, the Mexican beaded lizard, are the only known lizards in the world with venom glands. The Gila monster is seriously overrated as a threat to humans, however, because its venom apparatus is primitive and does not function like that of most venomous snakes, which inject venom through a pair of fangs. In 1999, after a methodical review of medical case histories, David Brown and Neil Carmony concluded that "no person in good physical condition and spared harmful or misapplied medical assistance has ever died from the bite of a Gila monster."

Stored in glands in the bulging lower jaw, the venom is released when the animal chews, prompting some scientists to conclude that the venom evolved as a defensive weapon for the slow-moving reptile. "It is impossible for such lizards to engage their jaws unless an attacker ventures within a few inches," Bogert and del Campo declare. "It follows that human beings are rarely bitten unless they have either attempted to capture these venomous lizards or have handled or malhandled captives."

The Gila monster has been maligned for its supposedly "homely" physical appearance, but if one judges the lizard by its distinctive colors and patterns (the markings "are never the same on two individuals," Brown and Carmony note), one might instead call it beautiful. True, the stout body and tail are sausage-shaped, the legs are chubby, and the head is thick and blunt, but the black marbling and contrasting pink, salmon, orange, or pale yellow hues of the skin's rounded tubercles resemble ornate beadwork. These designs are faithfully recreated in Native American art and basketry. The animal's tail is plump for a reason: it acts as a reservoir for the storage of fat. If denied food, a Gila monster can live "for many months upon the accumulated fatty tissue stored in the stumpy appendage," Ditmars says.

Residents of the Southwest once mistakenly believed this lizard lacked an anus (though they usually couched this "in much less delicate terms," Bogert and del Campo report), because the lizard's cloaca is concealed by scales. Since waste products therefore could not be eliminated in the customary manner, they presumably were "expelled through the mouth, where they contaminated the teeth," producing venom or "fetid breath" responsible for a hazardous "foul gas." *Scientific American* hypothesized in 1907 that desert heat "causes the food to putrefy in the stomach," but attempts to correlate the lizard's venom and "disagreeable odor" to a missing orifice were simply bad science.

Indigenous only to the American Southwest and to Mexico, Gila monsters are secretive and rarely seen; researchers estimate they spend up to 98 percent of their time below ground. Preferred habitats include shrubby deserts, rocky canyons and arroyos (water-carved channels), mountain slopes, oak woodlands, and nearby plains and beaches. As a rule, these reptiles are attracted to "somewhat moister" desert areas, Stebbins says, probably because their skin is permeable to water and therefore extremely susceptible to water loss. It absorbs water, too, which accounts for the many blissful hours that captive specimens spend soaking in pans of water.

Gila monsters, which grow to about 20 inches (50 cm) in total length, are primarily nocturnal, venturing from their underground burrows when temperatures moderate; occasionally individuals are encountered during daylight hours. Their cryptic coloration and disruptive skin patterns provide camouflage in dim light, Stebbins says, and by day the gaudy colors may serve as an aposematic warning to predators.

Since their diet consists largely of quail eggs and those of other birds and reptiles, some scientists question the evolutionary need for venom to subdue prey. (Rodents, however, are consumed on occasion.) In fact, these lizards are so passionate about eggs, slurping the contents with their large forked tongues, that they have been known to

Gila monster on fallen saguaro cactus
One of the world's two venomous lizards, the Gila monster of the American Southwest has a distinctive beadlike skin with a marbled pattern of salmon pink and black. Despite its stout, sluggish-looking body and short legs, the Gila monster can twist suddenly and lock its jaws onto a victim, holding on with the tenacity of a bulldog.

climb trees and cacti in search of nests. Other Gila monsters congregate beneath the perches of cliff-nesting birds.

The viciousness of Gila monsters is almost legendary: in the wild, they hiss and snap when disturbed, and the tenacity of their grip has inspired numerous comparisons to bulldogs. In extreme cases, Schmidt and Inger relate, pliers have been necessary to disengage the jaws.

During the mating season, males exhibit signs of territoriality, bobbing their heads and executing the signature lizard push-up; combat between rival males has been known to last for hours. When a receptive female is located, perhaps by her scent trail, she is courted by the male in a ritual that involves tongue flicking, rubbing his chin on her head, neck, or back, and nose nudging. Later, the female scoops out a hole in damp sand, where she lays a clutch of six to thirteen smooth, tough-shelled eggs.

"No biologist has yet discovered a Gila monster nest in the wild," Brown and Carmony report—an indication of just how secretive these creatures really are. The only reports of egg-laying refer to females in captivity.

Gila monsters are protected by law in Arizona, Nevada, Utah, New Mexico, and California, in an effort to curtail (if not fully prevent) their commercial exploitation. Whether skinned and stuffed, exhibited live in roadside zoos, or kept as contraband pets, these lizards have always exerted their own unique appeal. In the 1890s, according to Bogert and del Campo, a homeopathic practitioner conducted experiments on himself with Gila monster venom to ascertain its alleged powers as a medicine. After drinking a diluted solution of the venom, he reported feeling "an internal coldness from my heart" and, later, "sharp shooting pains in my bowels." He had also hoped to study the venom's rumored powers as an aphrodisiac but felt "too tired" to pursue that particular line of inquiry.

Other healers at the time conducted inconclusive experiments on the effect of the venom on patients with Parkinson's disease and advanced syphilis. A century later, in 2001, a neuroscientist at Thomas Jefferson University announced he had discovered a peptide in Gila monster saliva that dramatically improves memory retention in rats; he says he hopes his synthetic version, Gilatide, might boost memory receptors in the brains of humans suffering from Alzheimer's disease.

Eastern Glass Lizard

Ophisaurus ventralis

Horn snake. Joint snake. Glass snake. All are popular names for the same reptile, yet all are quite deceptive: *Ophisaurus* isn't a snake at all, it's a lizard—the longest lizard indigenous to the United States.

"It's hard to say which startles a person more," naturalist G. Earl Chace declares, "to find a snake that blinks or a lizard without legs." To the casual observer, all four species of North American glass lizards easily pass for snakes, since they are long and slender with no trace of legs. But they also have movable eyelids and well-developed ear openings, neither of which are found in snakes.

According to legend, these shiny creatures are made out of glass, and, when struck, their bodies break apart and their long tails "fly into pieces," Smith recounts. Afterwards, these "joint snakes" miraculously "reassemble" their body parts at the joints, Smith notes, and "rearticulate" the broken tail.

What makes such a feat seem remotely possible is the familiar escape maneuver called autotomy—intentionally breaking off the tail. The Eastern glass lizard has an exceptionally long and fragile tail, up to 2.75 times the head-body length; when grabbed by an enemy or intentionally cast off by the lizard, it appears to shatter. Later, after a new tail has grown, Chace says, the original point of breakage "is so obvious that it could easily be believed to have been put together again." Because the glass lizard's movements are unusually slow and stiff, such a defense tactic can be highly advantageous.

Other identifying characteristics of this species include distinctive eyelids and ear openings and a deep lateral groove or fold on each side of the body from the head to the base of the tail. This groove, herpetologists Roger Conant and Joseph T. Collins note, "permits expansion when the body is distended with food or with eggs." Adult Eastern glass lizards can reach a maximum overall length of 42⅝ inches (108 cm), but adults with unbroken tails average about 27½ inches (70 cm).

The ground color of the Eastern glass lizard is usually brown, black, or olive, with highly variable green dots or darker flecks on the sides and back that sometimes fuse to create stripes. "The ones I have seen," naturalist Olive Goin writes, "have been quite a light green in color, either striped or speckled in a way that gives them a curious checkered appearance." (The underside is white or greenish white.) Typically, juveniles are tan or khaki colored, with a broad stripe on each side of the body.

Prior to 1954, all glass lizards were classified as

Eastern glass lizard
Often mistaken for a snake, the limbless Eastern glass lizard is in fact America's longest native lizard. This reptile's upper surface is glassy and smooth, and when its brittle tail snaps off, observers say it looks like a "glass snake" being shattered.

Ophisaurus ventralis, but that year a scientist demonstrated there were actually three species; a fourth was described in 1987. The Eastern glass lizard is a resident of the Atlantic and Gulf coastal plains, ranging from Virginia (where Mitchell suspects it may have been introduced in bales of hay from the Carolinas) to Florida and west to Louisiana.

Glass lizards are commonly found in open fields, wet grasslands and meadows, coastal pine flatwoods, and hardwood hammocks, but because they are burrowing animals (often discovered during plowing), their behavior is not well understood. Some scientists report these lizards are active at night, but Carr has seen them sunning on boards and concrete, and Mitchell says they bask in the sun "with only part of their body exposed."

On collecting trips in the South, Ditmars concluded that glass lizards were nocturnal because so few were found by day—and because so many turned up in the early morning in wells, "where they had evidently tumbled during a nightly search for insects." Unlike snakes, these stiff and

"really clumsy" lizards could not escape without assistance. "Yet they were able to keep from drowning," Ditmars marveled, "by thoroughly inflating the lungs."

When handled, glass lizards often thrash about and attempt to bite their captor. Some also exude a foul-smelling substance and smear it on their antagonist. "This behavior," report Schmidt and Inger, "has been observed mainly as a reaction to one kind of enemy—herpetologists."

Glass lizards forage for insects, spiders, worms, slugs, snails, and snakes, and in captivity some resort to cannibalism. They also steal birds' eggs from nests on the ground, cracking the shells with their strong jaws and lapping up the contents with their large flat tongue.

Females engage in a behavior extremely rare for reptiles, rolling their body in a ring around their nest to brood their clutches of four to seventeen eggs. If startled, they may flee, returning later to regroup disturbed eggs with their snout.

119

Short-Horned Lizard

Phrynosoma douglasii

The horned lizard, better known to most Americans as the horned toad or horny toad, is short and stubby with rows of sharp spines on its sides and back and some pre-historic-looking spikes jutting from its head. Thus, it may seem odd that naturalist Jane Manaster calls the horned lizard "surprisingly charismatic." If not charismatic in the traditional sense, at least this doleful little creature from the "Old West" has a faithful following (the Horned Lizard Conservation Society); is the mascot of Texas Christian University and several high schools; and was once widely available at pet stores across the nation.

North America is home to all thirteen species of horned lizards, of which the short-horned lizard has the widest distribution—from southern Canada to central Mexico. This species is a native of fifteen states from the Pacific Northwest to the Texas Panhandle, where its habitats range from mountains and spruce-fir forests to short-grass prairies and sandy, semi-arid plains. The short-horned lizard is one of the smaller horned lizards, growing to 4⁵⁄₁₆ inches (10.8 cm) in length. The horns at the back of its head are shorter and stubbier than those of most other species, and it has a single row of "fringe scales" on each side of its body.

Individual short-horned lizards vary considerably in color—slate gray, brown, buff, beige, tan, reddish, or yellow, with dark blotches on the back and neck—but generally match their own environment. At higher elevations, where many are found, the short-horned lizard's cryptic ground color is often indistinguishable from the soil and rocks. Some individuals are "perfect imitations of the lichens covering the rocks," Ditmars says, while others are satiny black, mimicking the gloss on black lava.

This species is more cold-tolerant than most and, as a result, is the only ovoviviparous horned lizard in the United States. Females give birth to live young, which emerge from thin, transparent membranes deposited one at a time. Litters vary from five to thirty-six young, which "scurry over the ground with agility equal to the parent," Ditmars says, or burrow into the soil almost at once.

According to Manaster, young and adult horned liz-ards adopt one of three time-honored survival options when threatened: "Try to avoid detection" (i.e., hide); "If spotted . . . bumble off as fast as [possible]" (i.e., flee); and "Last, draw on a series of tactics to effect an alarming change" (i.e., attack). If the first and second options fail, the third may be embraced with remarkable zest. Pope recalls the flamboyant response of a short-horned toad he once encountered in Arizona: "The miniature monster puffed itself up, stood high on the tips of its toes, rocked its body back and forth, opened the mouth to reveal a dark lining, and finally hissed as it charged." The only antic it failed to resort to, he noted, was squirting blood from its eyes—a defense mechanism used by some horned lizards to startle, distract, or irritate a predator.

Another unusual characteristic of this lizard is its diet, which consists almost exclusively of ants. Short-horned lizards are ideally designed for catching ants, since they are flat, close to the ground, and have enormous stomachs; they are also patient sit-and-wait foragers, gobbling up swarms of ants as they file past in columns.

"Once within reach," writes Manaster, "the lizard will make a final spurt, thrust out its sticky tongue, swallow the mouthful alive, then retreat. . . . Yet when the situation is reversed, and ants attack a lizard, it will turn tail to escape because the ants can swarm the lizard and sting it to death." Recent invasions of fire ants from Brazil pose an environmental threat to horned lizards in parts of their range; the fire ants, scientists report, are decimating populations of red harvester ants that are a preferred food of these lizards (fire ants themselves are not eaten). Short-horned lizards also consume crickets, grasshoppers, beetles, butterflies, spiders, and snails.

One of the first Americans to write about short-horned lizards was explorer Meriwether Lewis, who noted in his expedition journal that the French called them "prairie buffalo," apparently because of the horns on their head (Lewis argued for the name "horned Lizzard" instead). The Hopi Indians before him were fascinated with these creatures and attributed to them powers of healing and fertility. Today, vendors of Native American art sell popular Zuñi-fetish stone carvings, or good-luck totems, in a wide array of animal shapes, including creative representations of horned lizards.

Short-horned lizard
Horned lizards are called "horned toads" by many people, but they are reptiles, not amphibians. The short-horned lizards of the Great Plains and American Southwest have short, stubby horns on their head and neck, and a row of fringe scales on their sides. When aroused, they puff up their body, hiss, and sometimes charge an intruder.

Eastern collared lizard

Recognized by its "neck collar"—a pair of black rings—this large North American lizard has a well-deserved reputation for pugnaciousness, sometimes biting without provocation. The Eastern collared lizard is agile and swift and can run on its hind legs alone, raising its front limbs off the ground.

Collared Lizard

Crotaphytus collaris

"Pugnacious" is the word most often used to describe the collared lizard of the American Southwest. Writers and collectors express frequent shock at this lizard's sudden transformation from appearing timid one moment to attacking and biting hard the next—"without any provocation and at every opportunity," Rogner insists. In fact, "their discrimination must be poor," Smith writes, "for they will act threateningly at almost any movement, when startled, whether the moving object be a dog, human, or train." To scare off intruders, a collared lizard opens its mouth and displays an intimidating black lining; if that fails, the lizard leaps from its perch and darts into a nearby crevice.

The Eastern collared lizard (also known, inexplicably, as the "mountain boomer," since it lacks a voice), can be identified by its double collar—two black rings around the neck, separated by white. The ground color is particularly striking during the breeding season—green, blue green, olive, straw yellow, or brownish—and herpetologist Brian Miller describes the males encountered during his childhood in Jefferson County, Missouri, as "absolutely gorgeous." Males also have a yellow or orange throat, and gravid females have red or orange spots or bars on the sides of the neck and body. (The Western collared lizard lacks the distinctive yellow-orange coloration on the throat.) Juveniles frequently have dark crossbands, which become less distinct as they age.

The collared lizard has a large, broad head, a short snout, and a long tail; it attains a maximum size, including tail, of about 14 inches (35.6 cm). The tail can grow to twice the length of the body, but it does not autotomize like tails of many other lizards. Particularly noteworthy are the powerful hind legs, which are up to three times the size of the front legs. When spooked, a collared lizard takes off running on all four legs, and, after gaining speed, it rises up on its hind legs "like a diminutive racing dinosaur," Smith marvels. The lizard is renowned for its leaping skills too: it rears up "in kangaroo fashion," writes Ditmars, and springs nimbly from rock to rock like a frog. The long, tapering tail helps the lizard to maintain its balance the same way a tightrope walker uses a pole, Barker explains.

Collared lizards eat like frogs too, stuffing food into a massive mouth using their front feet. Although they feed chiefly on grasshoppers, beetles, moths, spiders, and small lizards and snakes, collared lizards also eat berries, leaves, and the blossoms of red clover and dandelions. Roadrunners and snakes are their chief enemies.

The five subspecies of collared lizards range from Missouri to central California and southward into Mexico, inhabiting mountain slopes, canyons, gullies, limestone ledges, lava fields, and other rocky terrain. They bask atop boulders, from which they vigilantly survey their surroundings, but the boulders cannot be too large or too steep, Smith says, because these lizards are "not adept climbers."

Collared lizards are active by day and retreat to rocky crevices or burrows on overcast days and after sundown. Males are highly territorial and exhibit stereotypical aggression displays, flattening their body, standing high on their legs, and extending their throats.

When excited, courting males will bob their head up and down, rush the female, seize her neck in their jaws, and then copulate. Females lay one or two clutches of four to twenty-four eggs during the early summer months, depositing eggs in soft, paperlike shells in loose sand or in tunnels beneath rocks.

Six-Lined Racerunner

Cnemidophorus sexlineatus

"Racerunners deserve their name," declares herpetologist Christoph Scherpner; "they flit away in a flash, stop suddenly to look around for the enemy, and then dash off again." In 1941, the running speed of a racerunner was clocked at 18 miles (29 km) per hour, making it, according to Barker, "the fastest-moving of all North American reptiles." To herpetologist W. J. Breckenridge, however, 18 mph sounded "disappointingly slow"—until he calculated that for a "good-sized" police dog to travel this fast, with respect to its body length, "it would have to run nearly 300 miles an hour."

Clearly, the racerunner has earned its name, even though any races it hopes to win must be relatively short, due to its low metabolism. But the common designation "six-lined" can be puzzling to observers—not because the lizard's speed allows so little time to count all its stripes, but because authorities record the number of stripes variously as six, seven, or even eight.

Mathematical precision aside, the taxonomic classification too has "long baffled students," Pope remarks. "The variation exhibited by series of individuals is bewildering . . . [and] in most species a marked change in pattern begins soon after hatching and continues indefinitely." Another reason is the six-lined racerunner's tendency to interbreed with prairie racerunners.

Adult males are usually green, blue, or blackish in color; females and juveniles are more often brown. Narrow stripes of light yellow, white, cream, or pale gray line the back and sides, from the head to the base of the tail, then become less distinct. Many individuals have a broad brownish stripe down the center of their back. During the spring breeding season, males display bright blue or green on the sides of their glistening white belly. The lizard's tongue is black and forked.

Racerunners have a streamlined body with a narrow, pointed head, a long tapering tail, and strongly clawed toes. They attain a maximum length of about 9½ inches (24.1 cm), including the tail, which the lizard does not autotomize, Mitchell says, because of its usefulness in assisting with balance while running. (Other herpetologists disagree, reporting that it can detach its tail and generate a new one.)

Six-lined racerunners are commonly found east of the Mississippi River from Maryland south to the Florida Keys (though absent from the Florida Everglades and Mississippi River delta), west to eastern New Mexico, and as far north as South Dakota and Minnesota—a large range for a North American lizard. Racerunners are more inclined to wander than other lizards, Fitch says, and are "capable of traveling substantial distances, perhaps even several miles."

Sometimes called the field-streak, streak-field, or sandlapper, the six-lined racerunner is partial to well-drained open areas and dry, sandy habitats such as fields, barrens, road banks, dunes, and prairie hillsides. In Tennessee cedar glades, they are often found beneath slabs of limestone during the hottest part of the day, or in burrows where females lay their eggs. Six-lined racerunners live in colonies and are not territorial, although they do defend their burrows, and "frequent chasing and biting" are evidence of a "social hierarchy," the Burtons claim.

The standard mating ritual begins with the male wriggling his hindquarters in a figure-eight pattern, bringing his cloaca in contact with the ground, and then dashing toward nearby individuals—male and female. If he finds a receptive female, he attempts to straddle her back, and, "if she is responsive, he rubs his hip region against her back while nipping at her neck," Schmidt and Inger report. Males sometimes track females by their scent trail, according to Mitchell, and "forcibly mate with them, even digging them out of burrows to do so." Females deposit clutches of one to six thin-shelled eggs underground in sandy soil or tunnels, or beneath heat-absorbing rocks.

The oldest racerunner specimen in existence was collected in Virginia by none other than General George Meade, who was later named commander of the Union Army just before the Battle of Gettysburg. According to historian Franklin Tobey Jr., Meade collected the specimen in Richmond during the Seven Days' Battle and donated it to Harvard. The specimen has been floating in preservative in the Harvard Museum since 1862.

Fence Lizard

Sceloporus undulatus

The fence lizard, also known as the Eastern fence lizard, common swift, pine lizard, and prairie lizard, is sometimes called a "superspecies." It comprises ten or eleven subspecies (including the Northern and Southern fence lizards, Northern and Southern prairie lizards, and Northern and Southern plateau lizards), and members of the genus are collectively known as swifts or spiny lizards. There is also a Western fence lizard (Sceloporus occidentalis), with its own subspecies, but "no single [physical] characteristic known" separates the Eastern from the Western, according to Stebbins. Counting dorsal scales is one of the few reliable methods of distinguishing among these lizards.

Sceloporus is "perhaps the dominant lizard of the elevated, dry region of North America from the Southwestern United States through central Mexico," Pope observes, and although herpetologists debate the precise number of species and subspecies (about fifty), Schmidt and Inger joke that the spiny lizards "have their headquarters in Mexico," because the genus is so well represented there.

Like most spiny lizards, author Percy Morris observes, the Eastern fence lizard is "a shy creature, agile and swift," often seen perched on wooden fences. When startled by an intruder, a fence lizard darts up a tree and circles around to the back side to keep out of sight. But curiosity invariably gets the better of it, and the lizard edges back around the tree to peek at the trespasser; if detected, it will circle even higher and repeat the ritual.

Usually gray, brown, reddish bronze, or black, with crossbars or stripes on its back, the Eastern fence lizard blends in superbly with its surroundings—tree bark, pine forest or woodland floors, rocky slopes, sand dunes, prairies, and farmlands. (Melanistic populations have even been found in the vicinity of dark lava flows.) Male fence lizards sport blue patches on each side of the throat and on the sides of the belly; females may be yellow or reddish at the base of the tail. The striking cobalt-blue patches advertise the gender to other fence lizards—which scientists have confirmed in experiments by painting over the blue and watching these "de-sexed" males be treated as females by other fence lizards.

Adult Eastern fence lizards measure 4 to 7¼ inches (10 to 18.4 cm) in total length; females are generally larger than males. Primarily insectivores, they eat flies, moths, beetles, crickets, ticks, ants, spiders, millipedes, and snails. (In the West, gardeners report seeing fence lizards eat snapdragon blossoms and fallen rose petals.) Noted for

Fence lizard

A shy, swift lizard whose earth colors and markings afford excellent camouflage, the male fence lizard defends its small territory vigorously from other males. Often seen perched on a fence, bobbing its head and performing pushups when aroused, the fence lizard is a sit-and-wait predator, snatching moths and crickets and shaking them in its tiny jaws.

their keen eyesight, they can detect even very slight movement from a considerable distance. Most are sit-and-wait foragers, but once they capture their prey, they often shake it vigorously and crush it in their jaws.

Males are territorial, setting up small "fiefdoms" that they defend against other males. According to herpetologist Roger Barbour, one or two females may be found within a particular territory, "but they do not set up territories of their own." Females, however, are allowed to wander in and out of males' territories. After mating, females lay clutches of four to seventeen eggs in nests dug in well-drained sandy soil, sawdust, rotting wood, or even in the center of little-used country roads. The narrow white eggs turn dingy over time and hatch in about ten weeks.

Fence lizards overwinter in burrows and rocky crevices, under bark, and in other protected sites; in the spring, juveniles emerge earlier than adults and, in the fall, retire later. Predators include black racers, rat snakes, kingsnakes, and copperheads, as well as cats and dogs.

Curiously, these shy lizards can become tame enough to accept food from humans. "In my garden," says naturalist Frank Gander, "they would come into my hand to take mealworms, and if I sat in a chair near them, they would come and climb over me in hopes of being fed. . . . When I offer a mealworm in my hand, they look into my eyes before accepting or declining the bait. Those that refuse to come to me usually turn away so that the tail is pointing at me and then vibrate it very rapidly."

Granite spiny lizard
Partial to granite outcrops and rocky canyons, the granite spiny lizard of extreme Southern California and Mexico's Baja peninsula is a superb climber. Its scales are keeled and especially sharp on the tail, and the male's bright blue and purple markings give this lizard a strikingly colorful appearance.

Granite Spiny Lizard

Sceloporus orcutti

"This," declares Robert Stebbins, "is a wary lizard." He is not the only herpetologist to characterize the granite spiny lizard this way. A large (roughly 9¼ inches [23.5 cm], including tail), sharp-scaled species, this cautious creature inhabits the coastal side of peninsular mountain ranges from extreme southern California to the tip of Baja California and a few islands in the Gulf of California.

The lizard's celebrated wariness helps to compensate for its lack of camouflage, Stebbins argues; indeed, the granite spiny lizard is notorious for striking a pose atop rock formations, which makes the lizard perilously conspicuous. But when this rock-climbing reptile spots an adversary, it darts swiftly into a crevice, where the sharply pointed scales on its outward-facing tail make it difficult to dislodge. In late afternoon, however, these lizards sometimes become so preoccupied with their sunbathing that humans can stand within a few feet of them, Smith reports.

The granite spiny lizard is generally a coppery color, with a broad purple stripe down its back, a black shoulder patch (not pronounced in all males), and vivid blue or blue green on its throat and belly. In the center of each scale on its upper surface is a blue (or yellow-green) spot; on its flanks, smaller spots appear on each side of this spot. This is "one of our most beautiful lizards," Stebbins says of males clad in their bright blues and greens. Females generally lack the gaudy blue and purple of males, but their shoulder-patch crossbands may be more evident. Juveniles of both sexes have the pronounced crossbands, which alternate between dark rusty colors and lighter browns.

Favored habitats include arid or semi-arid rocky canyons with sufficient moisture to sustain oak, chaparral, mesquite, or palms; piñon-juniper woodlands; and subtropical thornforests. Granite spiny lizards prey on grasshoppers, cicadas, ants, beetles, and other insects, but also eat buds and fruits. Females lay clutches of six to fifteen eggs between the months of May and July.

Lava Lizards

Tropidurus

Lava lizards are one of only three genera of lizards that have found their way to the Galápagos Islands, leaving other *Tropidurus* species behind in tropical South America. Seven lava lizard species have been identified on the Galápagos archipelago: one each on six peripheral islands, and a seventh on the central and western islands. Unlike the considerably larger marine and land iguanas, lava lizards are small, ranging in length from 3 to 13½ inches (7.6 to 34 cm), including the tail.

Lava lizards are highly conspicuous, Galápagos tourists report, because they are plentiful and often brightly colored. Unlike many reptiles, male and female lava lizards sport different patterns and colors, which vary from island to island. The throats of females are generally bright red, while those of the larger males are black and yellow; youngsters are cryptically colored, and males do not assume their more intense colors until they mature. Many specimens are olive brown with greenish-gray flecks and black shoulder spots; populations inhabiting dark lava fields often have darker ground colors, while those living in sandy areas are lighter in color.

M. H. Jackson describes a "daily rhythm" adopted by lava lizards on the Galápagos Islands: on sunny mornings, they rise at dawn and sprawl on sun-warmed rocks to give their body temperature a quick boost. When the rocks become too hot, "one often sees lizards walking, or standing, on their 'ankles' with their toes raised off the ground to reduce heat transfer," Jackson notes. After seeking shelter during the hottest part of the day, lava lizards reappear in the late afternoon and remain active until dusk, when they hunker down for the night in loose soil or leaves.

Lava lizards habitually adopt lookout posts from which to survey their territories. Males bob their head and elevate their body in push-up fashion, employing rhythms and routines that vary from island to island. But lava lizards have evolved another curious ritual to discourage trespassers: a bloodless "ceremonial battle" in which they use their tails as weapons. Rivals face one another, reports Irenaus Eibl-Eibesfeldt, and nod their heads until "suddenly one of them rushes forward, stands alongside his opponent and lashes him with his tail once or several times." The lizards crack their whiplike tails "so hard that the blows can be heard several yards away." This ritual is repeated several times, sometimes by both males, until one abruptly abandons the field of battle and flees.

These reptiles eat primarily flies, moths, spiders, grasshoppers, ants, and scorpions; on islands where *Tiquilia* plants grow, lava lizards feast on the plant's flowers. Lava lizards are cannibals and will prey on youngsters of their own species. In turn, hawks, herons, mockingbirds, centipedes, and snakes all prey on lava lizards. Females lay three to six eggs at three- or four-week intervals during the warm season, depositing them underground in deep soil.

Lava lizard
Seven species of lava lizards live on the Galápagos Islands. Males survey their territories from preferred observation posts and challenge rivals with ceremonial fights that involve rushing an opponent and lashing him with the tail.

Green iguana
With its droopy dewlap, craggy head, and crest of spines, the green iguana of Central and South America resembles many an artist's fanciful rendition of a dinosaur or dragon. Hollywood filmmakers have exploited the resemblance by "casting" green iguanas as their extinct or mythical forebears and filming them in extreme close-up to exaggerate their size.

Green Iguana

Iguana iguana

The common green iguana—quite possibly the world's most recognizable lizard—boasts a high profile as a reptilian actor/model and popular household pet, but in some parts of the world its nickname reflects its fate on a dinner plate: *gallino de palo*, or "chicken of the tree." Unlike the "chicken of the sea," this hefty iguana is favored by many Central and South Americans, who find its flesh (and eggs) quite a delicacy.

The green iguana's range extends from southern Mexico to central South America, including several West Indian islands. But so many pet iguanas have escaped into the wild or been released by their owners after growing unmanageably long that they have established themselves in the United States—most notably in the Miami area, southern Texas, California, and Hawaii. Authorities report that feral iguanas are thriving in these locales and their populations are growing.

Equipped with long bodies and long whiplike tails, these lizards can grow to nearly 7 feet (more than 2 m) in total length and weigh as much as 18 pounds (8.2 kg). Green iguanas are easy to identify by their physical appearance: a row of dragonlike spines down the back, oversized dewlap and jowls, big round brown eyes, and a mouth that "gives the impression of being turned down slightly in a wistful cynical smile," Richardson says, "like that of the late Somerset Maugham in one of his mellower moods."

Hatchlings are usually bright emerald green, but older males may darken to golden orange and older females to olive, although colors and markings—including dark crossbars on the back—vary considerably. Some specimens from Peru are bluish or turquoise, while island populations are occasionally lavender or even pink.

The green iguana's favored habitat is a canopy of trees where it can bask on branches that hang over water. When disturbed, the seemingly nonchalant iguana will rouse itself from its lazy sprawl and dive into the water below, using its strong tail as an oar to swim effortlessly away. If not near water, it will simply crash to the ground, and, if the tree is host to a number of iguanas (which sometimes sleep in each other's arms or on top of one another), "the voyager often encounters quite a shower of falling iguanas," Hans Gadow wrote in 1901, "and runs some risk of getting his neck broken."

Iguanas inflict other injuries as well. Their long claws can leave a nasty scratch; their teeth can deliver a serious bite; and their muscular tail "can quickly put a dog out of action," remarks Werner Kästle, "with extremely accurate whiplashes." ("We have had our boots lashed by a cornered iguana in Guatemala," Schmidt and Inger write, "and we can attest to both the accuracy and force of the weapon.")

Despite their long claws and whiplash tail, green iguanas have become enormously popular pets in recent years; Mexican and South American "iguana farms" now harvest them for pet dealers, who imported more than 800,000 to the United States in 1995 alone. Nonetheless, experts warn, captive green iguanas are very difficult to care for and often die shortly after acquisition. In the wild, adult iguanas eat primarily flowers, leaves, and fruits (young iguanas eat insects), so pet owners are inclined to serve their iguanas lettuce—which can actually be harmful. "Because of its poor food value and the chemicals to which it may have been exposed," Rogner cautions, greenhouse lettuce "should not be given to these lizards."

Although some owners find iguanas to be docile and even attentive pets—one Philadelphia biology professor even claims his pet iguana can pick him out of a crowd, bobbing his head furiously when he sees and hears his master—many others eventually tire of the jaws and claws and prefer their iguanas on the big screen instead. These lizards have been stand-ins for dinosaurs and dragons in cheesy Hollywood movies for years. Iguanas are filmed close to the camera to exaggerate their size relative to human actors in the distant background and to emphasize their spiky spines.

While some iguana owners complain these animals devote most of their time to sleeping and eating, two German researchers, Hansjürgen Distel and J. Veazey, observed eight large iguanas in captivity for eighteen months and created a "behavioral inventory" of ninety-two different displays, postures, and other movements, including grooming, basking, fighting, defense, and mating.

Green iguanas are social animals, often found in groups; the territorial males engage in vigorous head bobbing, dewlap display, and push-ups to warn off intruders. In sandy soil, females lay clutches of up to seventy-one eggs, which hatch in about three months. In the 1970s, Gordon Burghardt of the University of Tennessee observed the behavior of hatchling iguanas on a small islet in Panama with fellow herpetologists Harry Greene and A. Stanley Rand. The young, he reported, dug "escape tunnels up to the surface," poked their heads out, and would "pop up and down repeatedly...looking for predators." The researchers were surprised to witness "synchronized emergence" from the holes: the hatchlings "usually leave in groups of two to eight, or as singletons followed shortly by another . . . like children leaving a party."

Marine Iguana

Amblyrhynchus cristatus

"It is a hideous-looking creature, of a dirty black colour, stupid, and sluggish in its movements," Charles Darwin wrote of the marine iguana after his famous voyage to the Galápagos Islands in 1835. Yet while repulsed by their physical appearance, Darwin was captivated by their behavior. The world's only marine lizards, these iguanas swim in frigid ocean currents and feed almost exclusively on red and green algae (Darwin discovered this after opening their stomachs). At that time, the lizards knew so little fear that when Darwin pitched one into the water, it returned repeatedly to the spot where he stood.

"Perhaps this singular piece of apparent stupidity may be accounted for by the circumstance, that this reptile has no enemy whatever on shore," Darwin concluded. (Scientists today speculate this individual probably had not warmed itself sufficiently in the sun to tolerate the freezing temperatures of the sea.) Nearly one hundred years later, explorer William Beebe said he found these iguanas so tame he was able to scrawl their scientific initials on one that crawled up beside him.

The lizard that "goes to sea in herds" and looks like "alligators in miniature," as Captain James Colnett described them in 1798, has another peculiar habit: at night, marine iguanas pile atop one another and sleep together (or "cuddle," as one herpetologist puts it), apparently to reduce loss of body heat in the cold night air. Today marine iguanas enjoy a protected status enforced by Ecuadorian and international authorities, so they may be studied only under carefully prescribed conditions ("even Darwin himself would now need a research permit," nature writer Quammen concedes).

Ecotourists who visit the Galápagos Islands often comment on how often these lizards sneeze and snort, perhaps fearing some sort of reptilian illness. Actually, the iguanas are expelling salt that has accumulated from high concentrations in their diet, Jackson explains. Since the salt glands are connected to their nostrils and located above the eyes, the resulting encrustation of expelled salt on the marine iguana's head is said to resemble an English barrister's wig.

Seven subspecies of marine iguana populate seven different islands of the Galápagos, some growing as long as 5.6 feet (1.7 m) and weighing as much as 20 pounds (9 kg). Sporting a prominent dorsal crest and tall protuberances atop their small, blunt head, marine iguanas boast strong claws (for gripping the rough volcanic rock), partially webbed feet, and a flattened, oarlike tail that facilitates swimming. These lizards bask leisurely in the sunshine, legs outstretched, until sufficiently warmed, then glide into the cold ocean waters and dive for seaweed. Females and juveniles prefer to eat the seaweed from nearby reefs that are exposed when the tide is out.

Not all marine iguanas, however, are strict herbivores. When Quammen visited painter Karl Angermeyer at his remote house on Santa Cruz Island, he was startled to see marine iguanas hanging vertically from the roof and walls. He was even more surprised to see the lizards stampede madly when Angermeyer signaled it was time for their daily snack of bread and rice.

Within each colony, the larger males establish individual territories, where they court females and challenge rivals during the breeding season. After displaying typical lizard postures to ward off intruders (erecting the crest, inflating the body, puffing out the throat, and bobbing the head), the more aggressive males will "butt, shove, and butt again," Quammen reports in *The Song of the Dodo,* "like a Tennessee roadhouse on a Saturday night."

After mating with a resident male, females often become aggressive toward other females and migrate to nearby "nesting territories," where they lay their eggs in sandy burrows and guard them warily for as long as sixteen days. The eggs incubate for a period of 89 to 120 days.

After studying Galápagos marine iguanas during two recent El Niño events (1990–95 and 1997–98), researchers Martin Wikelski and Corinna Thom discovered that individual specimens "became shorter by as much as 20%" in body length—shrinkage which, they hypothesized, was an "adaptive response" to "energetic stress" and low food availability. During this time, green and red algae disappeared and were replaced by hard-to-digest brown algae. Bone absorption, the researchers concluded, "accounts for much of the reduction."

More recently, after a tanker ran aground off San Cristobal Island in January 2001 and leaked some 170,000 gallons of oil, scientists initially believed the marine iguanas in the area would not be affected. But in June 2002 a team of ecologists reported that as many as 15,000 marine iguanas died on nearby Santa Fe Island in the year following the spill, perhaps due to disruption of intestinal bacteria that the iguanas rely on to digest algae.

Marine iguana
Found only on the Galápagos Islands, the marine iguana dives into cold Pacific waters to feed on algae. Returning to land, these iguanas sprawl on dark lava to warm their bodies in the sunshine and regulate their body temperature.

Galápagos Land Iguanas

Conolophus subcristatus, Conolophus pallidus

Darwin was as unimpressed with Galápagos land iguanas as he was with marine iguanas. "Like their brothers the sea-kind," he wrote, "they are ugly animals, of a yellowish orange beneath, and of brownish red colour above; from their low facial angle they have a singularly stupid appearance."

Land iguanas were far more plentiful in 1835 than they are today. Currently listed as threatened, these two species of land iguanas have been severely decimated by humans, goats, feral cats, and dogs on many of the Galápagos Islands, and populations on several islands are now extinct. One species, *Conolophus pallidus*, is found exclusively on Santa Fe Island; the other, *C. subcristatus*, is native to six islands. Some scientists believe *C. pallidus* is probably a "local variant," or subspecies, of the other.

Like their marine counterparts, land iguanas have a dorsal crest, but their tail is round rather than flat. Land iguanas grow to lengths of about 3.6 feet (1.1 m) and weigh 10 to 15 pounds (4.5 to 6.8 kg). Their head is "covered, or rather paved, with large cobblestone-like scales," Gadow writes, and the coloration of the stout body varies from mustard yellow to reddish brown, with unevenly distributed spots. According to Jackson, when these iguanas become excited, their colors brighten dramatically.

While marine iguanas graze on algae in the sea, adult land iguanas survive almost exclusively on a diet of prickly pear cactus (juveniles eat insects). "The mouths of these creatures must be incredibly tough," Jackson concludes, "as they may swallow cactus pads and fruits without removing the spines." Biologist Robert Rothman says it is "not unusual to see them sitting under a cactus, waiting for pieces to fall," and adds: "I once watched an iguana dislodge a thorn from its tongue by sticking its tongue out and dragging it back across its teeth several times." Darwin himself had some fun at the iguanas' expense by throwing pieces of cactus in their direction: "It was amusing to see them trying to seize and carry it away in their mouths, like so many hungry dogs with a bone."

Over time, Galápagos land iguanas, like giant Galápagos tortoises, have evolved a curious symbiotic relationship with birds: mockingbirds, small ground finches, and medium ground finches are allowed to pluck ticks and other parasites from the reptile's skin. Typically, says Jackson, a bird lands "on or near the iguana, which, if it wishes to be cleaned, takes up the 'cooperative' posture, raising itself off the ground as high as possible on all fours, remaining motionless while the bird removes ticks from the exposed skin."

Sexually mature male land iguanas defend territories that generally include several females. During the breeding season, the males bob their head, stamp their feet, and puff up their body and throat to intimidate other males. Should these aggression displays fail, the iguanas sometimes resort to bashing heads. A female signals her receptivity to mating with her posture and a scent trail; an interested male will follow the trail and circle around her until close enough to grab her neck in his jaws and restrain her during copulation. "After mating," Jackson says, "the female often flees from the male. I have seen females evade an ardent male's ministrations by sprinting at a surprisingly fast speed out of his territory."

Females and their mates may share a shallow burrow, constructed on level patches of soft sandstone or between fragments of lava, or they may live in adjoining burrows. "The holes do not appear to be very deep," wrote Darwin, "so that when walking over these lizard warrens, the soil is constantly giving way, much to the annoyance of the tired walker." Females deposit clutches of five to fifteen eggs in nesting burrows, which they defend from other females.

According to Rothman, male marine iguanas, "in a mating frenzy, occasionally attack and rape female land iguanas." DNA tests confirm that at least one iguana is the hybrid offspring of a male marine iguana and female land iguana, and researchers suspect there may be others.

Because of the continuing threat of extinction to island populations, the Charles Darwin Research Station and the Galápagos National Park Service have established the Reptile Rearing Center, a breeding center for land iguanas on Santa Cruz Island. The center has been instrumental in repatriating some 765 iguanas on three islands.

Galápagos land iguana
Two species of fat, mustard-colored land iguanas inhabit the Galápagos Islands, where they thrive on the succulent leaves and fruit of the prickly pear cactus.

Rhinoceros Iguana

Cyclura cornuta

Claiming that a rhinoceros iguana looks like its heavyset African or Asian mammalian namesake may be a bit of a stretch, but then there's the matter of the horns. Rhinos have one or two on their snout, and the rhinoceros iguana, not to be outdone, has three. Some observers think these three horny protuberances (variously described as conelike, pointed, rounded, stubby, and blunt) give the lizard a faintly sinister appearance; others, including Ditmars, say this lizard recalls the classic museum portraits of dinosaurs.

In addition to the three horns on the tip of the male's snout (females have rather inconspicuous protuberances), the rhinoceros iguana has a large, pendulous throat pouch, a saggy flap of skin on each side of the neck, and a crest of pointed scales running from behind the head to the end of the tail. These iguanas can grow quite large, attaining a total length of 28 to 48 inches (71 to 120 cm).

Restricted to islands of the Caribbean—Cuba, Hispaniola, Jamaica, the Bahamas, and the Cayman Islands—the three recognized subspecies of rhinoceros iguana face possible extirpation in some areas and are listed as threatened. Feral goats, dogs, cats, and pigs are chiefly responsible for the decline of this iguana, and habitat destruction caused by loggers and livestock owners has hastened its eradication. At one time, Haitians also hunted this animal for food.

The coloration of the rhinoceros iguana—gray, grayish black, brown, or olive brown—is "the perfect camouflage" for a ground-dweller that inhabits dry, rocky terrain, says Nashville Zoo Curator of Ectotherms Dale McGinnity. These iguanas are diurnal and live in burrows they dig in the rocky soil and coral of the islands.

All newly arrived specimens examined at the New York Zoological Park were "extremely vicious," Ditmars wrote in the early 1900s, "lashing the tail from side to side and rearing up on the hind legs in an effort to bite." Other herpetologists confirm that the tail can deliver quite a blow, including one witness who saw a rhinoceros iguana crush a metal watering can with its tail. Ditmars and other zookeepers note that this lizard has a curious habit of squatting on its hindquarters, bracing its front half on its strong front legs, and maintaining this position, looking "as motionless as if carved from stone."

Females dig tunnels to nest chambers where they lay eight to twenty-four eggs, sealing up the tunnels as they exit. In the wild, rhinoceros iguanas are omnivorous, preferring plants and berries but also eating insects, snails, rats, and other small animals. In captivity, their favorite foods include bananas, mashed potatoes, cooked rice—and sometimes their own offspring.

Rock iguana

Eight recognized species and several subspecies of rhinoceros iguanas (Cyclura) are found on the steppes and savannas of the West Indies. This Grand Cayman rock iguana (C. nubilia lewisi) is only slightly shorter than the better-known rhinoceros iguana C. cornuta, which is famous for the conelike protuberances on the male's snout.

Black Tree Monitor

Varanus beccarii

The taxonomy of New Guinea's black tree monitor has inspired many a scientific debate. What was once classified as a subspecies of the green tree monitor (*Varanus prasinus*) is today recognized by some, though not all, herpetologists as a distinct species. Also called Beccari's monitor (after the Italian explorer Odouardo Beccari), it is found only in humid forests and swamps of the Aru Islands off the southern coast of New Guinea.

Black tree monitors are handsome, slender, and entirely black, although hatchlings have rows of green or yellow spots that disappear within a few months. Growing to a maximum length of 37 inches (94 cm), including the tail, the black tree monitor has exceptionally long, strong limbs and sharp, needlelike claws—adaptations that enhance its dexterity as a climber. Extra support is provided by the long, prehensile tail, usually coiled when the lizard is at rest, which the lizard uses to grasp tree limbs and help brace the body.

Authorities say specimens caught in the wild are high-strung, extremely nervous, and flighty; some "run wildly for cover or leap off their perch at the first sight of an approaching intruder," Ruston Hartdegen reports. If handled carelessly, black tree monitors will scratch and bite, and may excrete the foul-smelling contents of their cloaca (a favorite defense tactic of numerous reptiles). Some black tree monitors are shy and will not eat in the presence of humans, but others learn to tolerate humans and even accept food directly from a keeper's hand. Black tree monitors sometimes develop an "incredible feeding response," Hartdegen notes, and will "leap upon their keepers in anticipation." In the mangrove swamps of New Guinea, black tree monitors eat crabs, frogs, and other small animals; in captivity, they eat insects, other invertebrates, and small mice.

During the breeding season, males pursue females, licking their neck and rubbing their chin across the female's body before copulating. Females often lay clutches of between two and six eggs twice a year. At the Dallas Zoo, keepers observed an aggressive female guard her nest by biting, lunging, slapping her tail, and inflating her throat. Hatchlings born in captivity have a relatively high mortality rate, perhaps due to unsuitable humidity levels or susceptibility to infections. Hartdegen considers these animals "intelligent," and zoogoers who have had a black tree monitor stare back at them for any length of time may have the eerie sensation that these lizards know something they don't know.

Gould's Monitor

Varanus flavirufus (formerly *Varanus gouldii*)

Named for John Gould, a nineteenth-century English naturalist who wrote about Australian wildlife, Gould's monitor is also popularly known as the sand monitor (or goanna) and the racehorse monitor/goanna. In Australia, monitor lizards are commonly called goannas, an apparent corruption of the word "iguana" that dates back to World War II, when American servicemen apparently confused the two families of large tropical lizards.

Like most monitors, this reptile has a long, slender body and tail and a very long neck. Reaching a maximum length of 5 feet (1.5 m), Gould's monitor has massive front legs; according to Sprackland, "it is disconcerting to see such a large lizard move so quickly" (which explains the name "racehorse monitor"). Careening off at top speed, it will frequently rear up on its hind legs and run bipedally. Another curious behavior is its habit of "tripoding"—rising on its hind legs and supporting itself with its tail to peer over tall bushes or rocks and scan its surroundings. Gould's monitor will also tripod when cornered, when grappling with a rival male, or when reaching for overhead branches. Australian herpetologist Raymond Hoser reports that irritated adult monitors will rise in a "kangaroo-like position" and hiss loudly.

The coloration of Gould's monitor often corresponds with its habitat: adults from red sandy deserts are frequently bright red, red brown, or yellow, while others may be tan, olive brown, dark brown, or black, with streaks, crossbands, or small scattered spots. Because of its "typical coating of dust and baked mud," this lizard's pattern is "often underestimated," Sprackland points out. Juveniles are generally brighter than adults.

Gould's monitor is not restricted to sandy deserts of the Australian interior; some populations inhabit coastal forests, and others are found in bushlands and jungle rivers. (Some authorities insist this species is averse to entering water, but others say it is a competent swimmer that

Black tree monitor
Equipped with long legs and toes, needle-sharp claws, and a prehensile tail, the black tree monitor is an expert tree climber. Zoo curators report that these strikingly dark-colored monitors are high-strung and shy, but surprisingly intelligent animals.

Gould's monitor
Gould's monitor is one of Australia's most common monitors. This ground-dwelling lizard forages over a wide territory, and, when it runs, it raises its front legs off the ground and dashes off bipedally on its rear legs, using its tail for balance.

remains submerged for short periods of time.) Gould's monitor is essentially a ground dweller, however, that is known for its burrowing skills. "If it has any failings," says Sprackland, "it is a poor climber, but it will scale tree stumps, fences, and even naturalists if that is what an escape route dictates."

Specimens in captivity have been characterized as quite intelligent, reportedly able to recognize individual humans and respond to given names. Sprackland says they are "frequent tail lashers" and may "cruise the glass" of their cages for years. In the wild, Gould's monitors are opportunistic feeders, scavenging on carrion and preying on small mammals, birds, insects, amphibians, and reptiles.

Females lay between five and twenty eggs in nests they excavate in sandy soil, decaying tree stumps, or termite nests. The termites apparently protect the eggs from predators, and the warmth and humidity of the nest accelerate development of the eggs.

Crocodile Monitor

Varanus salvadorii

The enormous size of New Guinea's crocodile monitor, or "tree crocodile," has intrigued herpetologists for years. Specific measurements are difficult to verify, but some believe this reptile is the longest lizard in the world. "Here is a mystery waiting to be explored," Sprackland declares; "unfortunately, unconfirmed reports of the exact size of this species are indicative of overall lack of knowledge about other aspects of its biology. . . . The New Guinea crocodile monitor may be the world's longest lizard, but so far no proof for that claim has been found."

Authorities at the Honolulu Zoo report that crocodile monitors grow to lengths of about 15 feet (4.6 m) from snout to tip of the tail; Sprackland places the upper limit at about 13.9 feet (4.2 m). In any event, the key to this monitor's presumptive record is its tail. According to Sprackland, the unusually long tail can approach 210 to 240 percent of the body length. That would mean a crocodile monitor with a body length (snout to vent) of 4 feet (1.2 m) would have an 8- to 9-foot (2.4- to 2.7-m) tail. Thus, while the Komodo dragon may be the world's "largest" lizard, due to its bulkier body and heavier weight, the crocodile monitor may well surpass the Komodo in length.

The scientific name for this lizard, *Varanus salvadorii* (honoring Italian ornithologist Tommaso Salvadori, who collected widely in New Guinea), contributes to the confusion surrounding this animal: *Varanus salvator*, the water monitor, is often mistaken for *salvadorii* because of similar-sounding species epithets.

That a lizard of such size would be a tree-dweller seems strange, but the crocodile monitor's long tail probably serves as a "counterbalancing appendage," Sprackland notes. Of course, it is also a handy defense weapon, and authorities at the Honolulu Zoo point out that, despite the creature's apparent docility, it can inflict "considerable damage" with its tail and tear human skin.

The crocodile monitor is found exclusively in Papua New Guinea, where it inhabits the upper canopy of lowland tropical forests. Long, sharp claws on long, thin limbs enable it to climb trees, where its narrow snout can pry beneath sheets of bark in search of prey, including insects, arthropods, and various small animals. "It is truly ironic," says Sprackland, "that the largest of lizards eats the tiniest of foods."

The crocodile monitor's skin is usually black, with flecks or rows of white dots across the back. Natives of New Guinea have traditionally hunted these monitors for their smooth skin, which they use to make drums.

Like Gould's monitor, this reptile rises up on its hind legs to survey its surroundings, a habit that some natives believe enables the animal to watch for crocodiles. (If it sees one, they claim, it issues a "warning call.") For decades, islanders feared this species was venomous, because bites sometimes led to human fatalities; these deaths, however, were apparently caused by infections from bacteria that thrive in the lizard's mouth, like those found in the mouth of the Komodo dragon.

"Monitor lizards are basically boring, phlegmatic animals."

—*Dale Marcellini (Curator, National Zoo)*

Crocodile monitor
The long head and narrow snout of the crocodile monitor may have evolved to seek out insects and other small prey beneath the bark of trees in the tropical forests of Papua New Guinea. Some experts suspect these monitors may exceed Komodo dragons in length, but no record-setting individuals have been measured and verified.

Komodo Dragon

Varanus komodoensis

When author David Quammen arrived on the Indonesian island of Komodo in search of the world's largest lizard, he enlisted a local ranger to help him find one in the wild, far away from the spectacles involving sacrificial goats staged for "doltish tourists." The two men followed a set of Komodo tracks through the forest, he recalls in *The Song of the Dodo,* and emerged into a sunlit savanna.

"Komodo!" ranger David Hau shouted suddenly.

Quammen continues: "We notice a commotion just ahead in the brush. Then a very large Komodo breaks into view, spooked by our trespass, and scrambles straight up the vertical face of the bluff, like an alligator scaling a four-story building. . . . At that moment I hear David scream as another big Komodo charges out of its hiding place just behind us.

"Yaaaggh. We whirl, caught flat.

"But this animal makes a split-second decision against cutting us off at the knees. Instead of snatching a mouthful of my buttocks or biting away David's left calf, it has peeled a sharp turn and set off downhill, moving as discreetly as a rhinoceros."

Close call. A slab of buttocks or chunk of calf is small potatoes to a lizard that can weigh up to 550 pounds (250 kg), depending on what's in its stomach, has a reputation as a mankiller, and harbors some fifty strains of bacteria in its mouth—some fatal to humans.

For a lizard that looks like a dinosaur, it is ironic that the Komodo dragon is so recent a discovery. In the early 1900s, colonial administrators launched an investigation after a Dutch pilot crashed on an island where, he reported, "prehistorical" dragons lurked. A Dutch army officer then found and killed a 6-foot 11-inch (2.1 m) specimen and sent a photo with the skin to a zoo in Java, which mounted an expedition that killed two more specimens and captured two juvenile lizards. In 1912, the zoo director published a paper announcing the discovery to the world.

Komodo dragon
First discovered in 1910 on an isolated island in Indonesia, the massive, prehistoric-looking Komodo dragon is believed to be the world's largest living lizard. As juveniles these monitors are shy and nervous, but as adults they can be aggressive and have been known to attack and even kill humans.

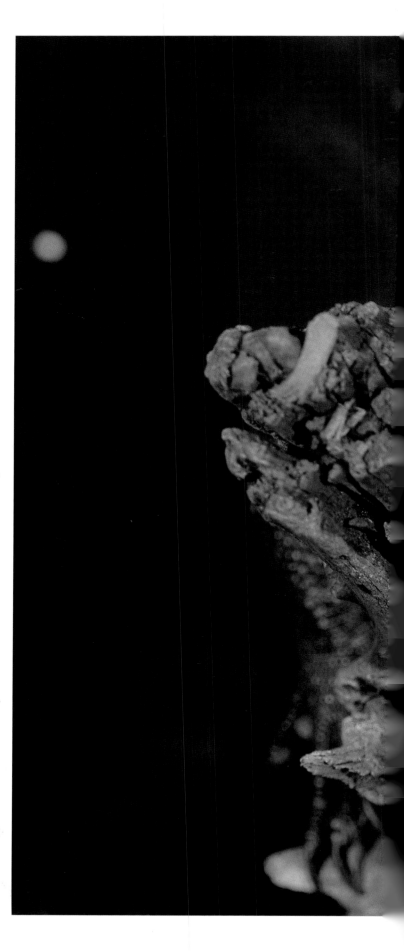

Many expeditions to Komodo and its neighboring islands followed, but the Dutch colonial government recognized the rarity of the beast and implemented plans for its protection. Today, Komodo dragons—of which there are no more than about 5,000 in the wild—can only be exported as a "state gift" with the blessings of the president of Indonesia.

Called "oras" by natives, Komodo dragons are uniformly clay colored, although juveniles may be dull brown or chestnut with a lime-green neck and chest and patches of orange on the shoulders and back. The long forked tongue, which constantly probes the air and ground for scent particles, is bright yellow.

The lizard's rough, scaly skin hangs loosely over its body, "like chain mail, gathering to a series of cowl-like folds just behind its long death's head of a face," an apprehensive Douglas Adams wrote after visiting Komodo Island. "Its legs are thick and muscular, and end in claws such as you'd expect to find at the bottom of a brass table leg. . . . It is massive to a degree that is unreal." (It also has "the worst breath of any creature known to man," coauthor Mark Carwardine added.)

Walter Auffenberg, the leading authority on Komodos, says that the "great size and weight" of adult oras, their "highly specialized teeth for slicing flesh," "high locomotor facility," and unusual predation habits contribute to the species' uniqueness. According to Auffenberg, the record length of the Komodo dragon is 10 feet 2½ inches (3.1 m) from snout to tip of the tail, and the average weight is about 104 pounds (47 kg), depending on whether the ora has recently eaten. "Feeding oras," he says, "eat prodigious amounts of food—up to 80 percent of the total weight of the empty ora."

The lizard's diet consists of deer, goats, and smaller prey, including their bones, hooves, and hide. Oras are scavenger-predators and pile onto a rotting carcass "like NFL linemen attacking a fumble," Quammen reports. Up to 10 percent of an adult's diet is young oras, which accounts for the youngsters' defensive habit of climbing trees to escape their cannibalistic elders. Another survival tactic is to roll in fecal matter, "thereby assuming a scent that their bigger brethren are programmed to avoid consuming," zoologist Claudio Ciofi explains.

Because much of this reptile's fearsome reputation is based on claims that it has attacked and killed humans, Auffenberg and others have endeavored to verify these incidents. Years ago, oras would "exhume recently buried human bodies" from sandy graveyards, Auffenberg learned, and he cites evidence of several confirmed deaths attributed to loss of blood after a severe bite or to virulent bacteria in the ora's saliva.

That oras are not afraid of humans became apparent during Auffenberg's extensive stays on the island. On one occasion, an ora entered a blind, "smelling my paper as I continued to write my notes, and moved my pencil all about. His 'curiosity' in the paper, the pencil and my hand was truly surprising." When Auffenberg moved to stand up, however, the dragon lumbered out of the blind.

Although this bulky beast looks sluggish, it can run remarkably fast, achieving speeds of up to 12.4 miles (20 km) per hour, according to Ciofi. If its prey climbs out of reach, an ora will stand on its hind legs and use its tail for support, like the third leg of a tripod.

During the mating season, adult males face off in an upright position and wrestle their rivals, sometimes drawing blood. The victor nudges and licks a receptive female (which she sometimes reciprocates), then crawls on his partner's back and manipulates his cloaca into position. The female will deposit her eggs in a hollow she digs or in the nest and may lie atop the nest during the eggs' eight-month incubation period. Adult Komodos often form "pair bonds," a behavior that Sprackland calls "rare in lizards."

In captivity, some oras apparently become tame; according to herpetologist Arthur Loveridge, a 7-foot (2.1-m) specimen in the London Zoo would permit its keeper to grasp its tail "and use it as a steering rudder on their walks about the premises." In June 2001, however, a large Komodo dragon at the Los Angeles Zoo attacked the shoeless foot of the *San Francisco Chronicle*'s executive editor, who was being treated to a private tour of the lizard's quarters as a gift from his wife, actress Sharon Stone. His big toe was crushed, and surgery was required to reattach several tendons, along with treatment for possible bacterial infection.

At the National Zoo in Washington, D.C., a pair of oras given to the United States in 1988 produced the first offspring born in captivity outside Indonesia; since then, zookeepers have had repeated success with breeding efforts. Despite the scarcity of these reptiles in collections around the world, the National Zoo's curator of reptiles, Dale Marcellini, says he hopes to make Komodo dragons "so common in zoos that they become boring really quick."

Reproduction of Komodo dragon nest and eggs
The National Zoo in Washington, D.C., is one of only a few selected zoos in North America where Komodo dragons are on display. This reproduction of a Komodo dragon's nest and eggs is based on the zoo's successful breeding program, which has produced several generations of hatchlings, including the first Komodo dragon hatched in captivity outside Indonesia.

"The lizard was simply going about its lizardly business in a simple, straightforward lizardly way. It didn't know anything about the horror, the guilt, the shame, the ugliness that we . . . were trying to foist on it."

—*Douglas Adams and Mark Carwardine,* Last Chance to See, *1990*

Chapter 4

Lizard Conservation

While collaborating on *Frogs* for Voyageur Press in 1994, John Netherton and I came across mounting scientific evidence suggesting that populations of amphibians around the world are in serious decline. Since then, mainstream media have spread this message, reporting anecdotal as well as empirical evidence of population declines and physical deformities in frogs.

When we began work on our next book, *Snakes*, we discovered that threats to reptiles are real, too; unfortunately, efforts to census populations of reptiles are complicated by the secretive nature of the beast. Forty years ago, herpetologist Archie Carr warned that "snakes are probably disappearing at a more rapidly rising rate than any other group of vertebrates," although he could offer little proof beyond personal observations.

Now, however, ecologist Whit Gibbons and ten coauthors of a study in *BioScience* have sounded a similar concern. "The disappearance of reptiles from the natural world is genuine and should be a matter of concern not simply because of reptiles' perceived associations with amphibians, but because reptile declines . . . are growing and serious in their own right," the authors declare. "Current evidence suggests that amphibian and reptile declines, which are exacerbated by burgeoning human populations, constitute a worldwide crisis."

That's chilling news—so why aren't warnings of this crisis more prevalent? The explanation, Gibbons and his coauthors suggest, is the "clandestine nature of many reptiles," which, along with their "comparatively large home ranges, low population densities, and rareness of congregational behavior," hampers long-term monitoring of population trends. Gibbons and his coauthors identify six principal threats contributing to the crisis and placing reptiles "in even greater danger of extinction worldwide" than amphibians: (1) destruction and degradation of habitat; (2) introduction of invasive species; (3) pollution; (4) disease and parasites; (5) unsustainable harvesting; and (6) climate change. All have had an impact on lizards in the United States and elsewhere.

Green anole
This green anole, photographed in silhouette on a palmetto frond, displays its agility as a climber. Although many lizards disappear when humans overrun their habitats, green anoles coexist easily with humans and are often glimpsed on fences, windows, and ornamental plants. In New Orleans, green anoles are so tame they will run up the outstretched arms of patrons dining in courtyards.

"If the world goes on the way it is going it will one day be a world without reptiles. Some people will accept this calmly, but I mistrust the prospect. . . . If we let the reptile go it is a sign we are ready to let all wilderness go. When that happens we shall no longer be exactly human."

—*Archie Carr,* The Reptiles, *1963*

Threats to lizard habitats are omnipresent and inescapable: urban expansion, suburban sprawl, commercial development, road construction, deforestation, burning, overgrazing, draining, and damming. Degradation or wholesale destruction of habitat not only extirpates local lizard populations, it also fragments breeding ranges and creates barriers to dispersal. This, in turn, affects reproductive behavior, producing smaller breeding pools that encourage genetic inbreeding, hybridization, and greater susceptibility to disease.

Introduction of invasive species can wreak havoc, too, since many prey on native species and compete with them for food. The brown tree snake, for example, encountered no natural enemies when accidentally introduced to Guam during World War II; it has been decimating gecko and skink populations (as well as native birds) ever since. In countries where "exotic" species of iguanas and geckos have escaped or been released, some encroachers prey on smaller lizards and compete for other resources.

Pollution, one of the best-known threats, impacts individuals, local populations, habitats, and entire ecosystems. Toxic chemicals and wastes drain into streams and lakes, poisoning drinking water and killing aquatic food sources; other pollutants contaminate the soil and leach into the water table. Pesticides, herbicides, fungicides, and chemical fertilizers run off into streams and lakes, disturbing aquatic ecosystems and leaving high concentrations of fat-soluble contaminants such as mercury, heavy metals (lead and copper), and dioxins, which accumulate in the food web, reduce the prey base, and cause abnormal development of animals and eggs. Emissions from smokestacks and vehicles contribute to acid rain and snow and increase mortality rates of lizards and other wildlife.

Parasite infestations and diseases are concerns as well. While amphibians have been the hardest hit (a parasitic chytrid fungus is believed responsible for recent die-offs of frogs in scattered parts of the world), lizards and other reptiles are also susceptible to debilitating or fatal diseases. In captivity, lizards succumb to metabolic bone disease, mouth rot, respiratory infections, mite and tick infestations, and fungal and bacterial infections.

As a result of unsustainable harvesting practices, populations of green iguanas, tegus, monitors, and other lizards have been decimated by humans who hunt these reptiles for their skins or for food and "medicines." In addition, to meet increasing demand for lizards of all types, the international pet trade depends on legal (and illegal) importation, as well as reptile farming and ranching programs. ("Tropical fish used to outnumber reptiles twenty to one," says Cornell herpetologist Kraig Adler, "but now they're neck and neck.")

Finally, climate change—global warming and alteration of temperature and precipitation patterns—and natural catastrophes, such as drought, floods, hurricanes, typhoons, earthquakes, and forest fires, can claim heavy, if unrecorded, tolls on the world's herpetofauna.

In the end, of course, the greatest threat to lizards is man. Although humans are not as phobic about lizards as they are about snakes, they routinely crush lizards with their cars, trucks, and off-road vehicles; strip off lizard skins to make boots, belts, purses, and wallets; melt down their fat for liniments and assorted "health" products; consume their flesh or grind it into powder (iguana soup and stew are traditional fare in Central America during Easter week); and collect them in the wild to sell or take home as pets.

In recent decades, environmentalists have come to the defense of threatened and endangered species of wildlife around the world—especially "charismatic megafauna" such as pandas, tigers, and whales—but the lowly lizard receives nowhere near the attention that is showered upon more prominent animals. The Convention on International Trade in Endangered Species of Wild Fauna and Flora (CITES) currently recognizes some sixteen endangered and sixty-six threatened species of lizards, of which fifty are "Red-Listed" (highlighted for their relative risk of vulnerability on a global scale) by the International Union for the Conservation of Nature and thirty-seven are protected by the U.S. Endangered Species Act.

In the United States, conservation of native herpetofauna is promoted by Partners in Amphibian and Reptile Conservation, the Society for the Study of Amphibians and Reptiles, and other organizations. One of the more active groups in the West and Southwest is the Horned Lizard Conservation Society, founded in 1990. In Great Britain, the Herpetological Conservation Trust has rallied to the defense of the threatened sand lizard and supported a species recovery program to safeguard its habitat. In the Canary Islands, where six specimens of the giant lizard *Galliota gomerana*, presumed extinct for some 500 years, were recently discovered, the reptiles are being cared for at the University of La Laguna before they are reintroduced into protected areas.

Leopard gecko
Leopard geckos, indigenous to many Asian countries, have become popular pets among herpetoculturists; today, they are among the most frequently bred gecko species in captivity.

In the Caribbean, where the Jamaican iguana and other iguana species have been declared "the most endangered lizards in the world" by the World Conservation Union, scientists and curators from six American zoos are cooperating to tag and track iguanas with miniature radio transmitters, control their predators, preserve their habitats, and sponsor captive-breeding programs. The Nashville Zoo's curator of ectotherms, Dale McGinnity, has initiated a conservation program to survey and study four species of Haitian giant galliwasps and is currently breeding captive specimens to create a "genetically viable" reserve population at the zoo. (Six of the eight females he collected have already given birth.) Captive-breeding programs at the Charles Darwin Research Station in the Galápagos Islands are increasing the world's population of land iguanas, and scientists and volunteers at Komodo National Park are committed to preserving the imperiled population of rare Komodo dragons.

One reason the public should be concerned about the future of threatened—and nonthreatened—lizards is purely selfish: certain species offer valuable economic and environmental benefits. Lizards have long been recognized as a source of insect control, especially in the tropics; sugarcane growers in Puerto Rico, for example, consider them highly beneficial. Slow worms are prized throughout Europe and Great Britain, where they control slugs in gardens and farmlands, and in Malaysia, monitor lizards are valued for devouring crabs that undermine dikes.

The prospect of lizards providing medical cures for humans has tantalized researchers for decades. The venom of Gila monsters, for example, harbors a substance called exendin, which stimulates secretion of insulin and "may one day be used to prevent the progression of diabetes," says ethnobotanist Mark J. Plotkin. The astonishing array of more than fifty strains of bacteria in the saliva of Komodo dragons tantalizes McGinnity and others, who believe antimicrobial peptides in these monitors offer a promising lead for pharmaceutical research. "When they eat," McGinnity notes, "their gums bleed, so bacteria get into their blood—but they aren't getting sick. Now *that's* interesting." McGinnity says that giant galliwasps offer medical promise too, as they have developed "unique molecular strategies" to deal with their toxic prey (millipedes, centipedes, spiders, etc.); a better understanding of galliwasps' interaction with toxins, he says, "could benefit man in the future."

Currently, the blood of the Western fence lizard is being evaluated for its role in the life cycle of Lyme disease. This lizard's blood contains a substance—"probably a kind of heat-sensitive protein," says researcher Robert Lane—that kills the bacterium in infected Western black-legged ticks that causes Lyme disease. "Lizards," he observes, "are doing humanity a great service here in the West."

Clearly, the conservation of lizards merits more urgent attention, and educators, journalists, biologists, and policymakers must assume greater responsibility for informing the public about the vital role of lizards—and the fragility of their ecosystems—around the globe.

"Students often ask me about a variety of organisms, so I am familiar with the questions 'Why conserve lizards? What good are they?'" reflects herpetologist Brian Miller. "These types of questions have no simple answers; only those unfamiliar with lizards could ask such questions.

"So I always suggest they get to know some local lizards. Marvel at the ability of a collared lizard to elude capture from a roadrunner or small boy as it races bipedal across an Ozark glade. Or watch a basilisk run bipedal across the surface of a Mexican stream. Listen to a banded gecko squeak when touched; or become frustrated by whiptail lizards leisurely dining on ants while you're in hot pursuit."

Education, insists Miller, is the only solution—education that comes not from "flashy" television programs but, rather, from observing lizards in their native environment.

"Request local schools to re-establish natural history studies and build ponds and other natural areas," he urges, "and balk at educational philosophies that rely on games to teach ecology. Use nature. Only through education and experience will people appreciate lizards. And only when they appreciate lizards will they finally become concerned about conserving them."

Central American banded gecko
Although there are more than 800 species of geckos worldwide, only six are native to the United States (others, however, have been introduced accidentally or intentionally). Most geckos are found in tropical or subtropical regions, including this Central American banded gecko.

"You walk among clattering four-foot marine iguanas heaped on the shore lava, and on each other. . . . The enormous land iguanas at your feet change color in the sunlight, from gold to blotchy red as you watch. There is always some creature going about its beautiful business."

—*Annie Dillard*, Teaching a Stone to Talk, *1983*

Swallow-tailed gull and marine iguana
Ecotourists flock to the Galápagos Islands every year to glimpse the unusual species of iguanas, tortoises, and birds that once fascinated Charles Darwin—but recently, spills from leaking oil tankers have harmed seabirds and marine iguanas.

Bibliography

Adams, Douglas, and Mark Carwardine. *Last Chance to See.* New York: Harmony Books, 1990.

Albert, Magnus (Albert the Great). *Man and the Beasts.* Vol. 47. Trans. by James Scanlan. Binghamton, N.Y.: Medieval & Renaissance Texts & Studies, 1987. Orig. published c. 1280.

Arnst, Catherine. "Gila Monsters: Can They Sharpen Your Memory?" BusinessWeek Online (September 24, 2001), www.businessweek.com/magazine.

Auffenberg, Walter. *The Behavioral Ecology of the Komodo Dragon.* Gainesville: University Presses of Florida, 1981.

Autumn, K., and Robert J. Full. "Adhesive Force of a Single Gecko Foot-Hair." *Nature* 405 (June 2000): 681–685.

Barbour, Roger W. *Amphibians and Reptiles of Kentucky.* Lexington: University Press of Kentucky, 1971.

Barker, Will. *Familiar Reptiles and Amphibians of America.* New York: Harper & Row, 1964.

Bartlett, R. D., and Patricia P. Bartlett. *Chameleons.* Hauppauge, N.Y.: Barron's, 1995.
———. *Geckos.* Hauppauge, NY: Barron's, 1995.
———. *Monitors, Tegus, and Related Lizards.* Hauppauge, N.Y.: Barron's, 1996.
———. *Anoles, Basilisks, and Water Dragons.* Hauppauge, N.Y.: Barron's, 1997.

Basey, Harold E. *Discovering Sierra Reptiles and Amphibians.* Yosemite National Park, Calif.: Yosemite Association, 1976.

Bauer, Aaron M. "Lizards." In *Encyclopedia of Reptiles and Amphibians,* 2d ed., edited by Harold Cogger and Richard Zweifel. San Diego: Academic Press, 1998, 126–73.

Bellairs, Angus. *The Life of Reptiles.* New York: Universe Books, 1970.

Bellairs, Angus, and Richard Carrington. *The World of Reptiles.* New York: American Elsevier Publishing Co., 1966.

Blair, W. Frank. *The Rusty Lizard: A Population Study.* Austin: University of Texas Press, 1960.

Bogert, Charles M. "The Lizards." In *The Animal Kingdom,* vol. II, edited by Frederick Drimmer. New York: Greystone Press, 1954, 1282–1322.

Bogert, Charles M., and Rafael Martín del Campo. *The Gila Monster and Its Allies.* Oxford, Ohio: Society for the Study of Amphibians and Reptiles, 1993. Orig. published 1956.

Brattstrom, Bayard H. "The Evolution of Reptilian Social Behavior." *American Zoologist* 14:1 (winter 1974): 35–49.

Breckenridge, W. J. *Reptiles and Amphibians of Minnesota.* Minneapolis: University of Minnesota Press, 1944.

Breland, Osmond P. *Animal Life and Lore.* New York: Harper & Row, 1963.

Broadley, Donald G. "Girdle-Tailed Lizards." In *Grzimek's Animal Life Encyclopedia,* vol. 6, edited by Bernhard Grzimek. New York: Van Nostrand Reinhold, 1975, 265–73.

Brown, David E., and Neil B. Carmony. *Gila Monster: Facts and Folklore of America's Aztec Lizard.* Salt Lake City: University of Utah Press, 1999.

Burghardt, Gordon M. "Of Iguanas and Dinosaurs: Social Behavior and Communication in Neonate Reptiles." *American Zoologist* 17:1 (winter 1977): 177–90.

Burghardt, Gordon M., and A. Stanley Rand, eds. *Iguanas of the World: Their Behavior, Ecology, and Conservation.* Park Ridge, N.J.: Noyes Publications, 1982.

Burton, Maurice, and Robert Burton. *Encyclopedia of Reptiles, Amphibians & Other Cold-Blooded Animals.* London: Octopus Books, 1975.

Capote, Truman. *Music for Chameleons.* New York: Random House, 1980.

Carmichael, Pete, and Winston Williams. *Florida's Fabulous Reptiles & Amphibians.* Tampa: World Publications, 1991.

Carpenter, Charles. "Aggression and Social Structure in Iguanid Lizards." In *Lizard Ecology: A Symposium,* edited by William Milstead. Columbia: University of Missouri Press, 1967, 87–105.

Carr, Archie. *The Reptiles.* New York: Time-Life Books, 1963.
———. *A Naturalist in Florida: A Celebration of Eden.* Edited by Marjorie Harris Carr. New Haven, Conn.: Yale University Press, 1994.

Cejudo, Daniel, and Rafael Márquez. "Sprint Performance in the Lizards *Gallotia Simonyi* and *Gallotia Stehlini* (Lacertidae): Implications for Species Management." *Herpetologica* 57:1 (March 2001): 87–98.

Chace, G. Earl. *The World of Lizards.* New York: Dodd, Mead, 1982.

Cherry, Jim. *Loco for Lizards.* Flagstaff, Ariz.: Northland Publishing, 2000.

Ciofi, Claudio. "The Komodo Dragon." *Scientific American* 280:3 (March 1999): 84–91.

Cloudsley-Thompson, John L. *Predation and Defense Amongst Reptiles.* Bristol, England: Longdunn Press, Ltd., 1994.

Cogger, Harold. *Reptiles and Amphibians of Australia.* Ithaca, N.Y.: Cornell University Press, 1994.

Cogger, Harold, and Richard Zweifel, eds. *Encyclopedia of Reptiles and Amphibians.* 2d ed. San Diego: Academic Press, 1998.

Cohn, Jeffrey P. "Indonesian Treasure Has a Jurassic Appeal." *BioScience* 44:1 (January 1994): 4–7.

Cole, Charles J. "Unisexual Lizards." *Scientific American* 250:1 (January 1984): 94–100.

Conant, Roger, and Joseph T. Collins. *A Field Guide to Reptiles and Amphibians of Eastern and Central North America.* 3d ed. expanded. Boston: Houghton Mifflin, 1998.

Crews, David, Jill Gustafson, and Richard Tokarz. "Psychobiology of Parthenogenesis." In *Lizard Ecology: Studies of a Model Organism,* edited by Raymond Huey, Eric Pianka, and Thomas Schoener. Cambridge, Mass.: Harvard University Press, 1983, 205–31.

Daan, Serge. "Agamids and Chameleons." In *Grzimek's Animal Life Encyclopedia,* vol. 6, edited by Bernhard Grzimek. New York: Van Nostrand Reinhold, 1975, 205–41.

Darwin, Charles. *Voyage of the Beagle.* New York: Collier & Son, 1956. Orig. published 1839.

DeCourcy, Kristi R., and Thomas A. Jenssen. "Structure and Use of Male Territorial Headbob Signals by the Lizard *Anolis carolinensis.*" *Animal Behaviour* 47:2 (February 1994): 251–62.

Degenhardt, William G., Charles W. Painter, and Andrew H. Price. *Amphibians and Reptiles of New Mexico.* Albuquerque: University of New Mexico Press, 1996.

de la Cepede, Count. *The Natural History of Oviparous Quadrupeds and Serpents.* Vols. I and II. Trans. by Robert Kerr. New York: Arno Press, 1978. Orig. published 1802.

de Vosjoli, Philippe, and Frank Fast. "Natural History, Captive Husbandry and Breeding of the New Caledonia Crested Gecko, *Rhacodactylus ciliatus,* Part 1: Natural History." *Vivarium* 10:6 (October–November 1999), 6, 8–9.

Distel, Hansjürgen, and J. Veazey. "The Behavioral Inventory of the Green Iguana, *Iguana iguana.*" In *Iguanas of the World,* edited by Gordon M. Burghardt and A. Stanley Rand. Park Ridge, N.J.: Noyes Publications, 1982, 252–70.

Ditmars, Raymond L. *Reptiles of the World.* Rev. ed. New York: Macmillan, 1933.
———. *The Reptiles of North America.* Garden City, N.Y.: Doubleday & Co., 1936.

Eibl-Eibesfeldt, Irenaus. "The Fighting Behavior of Animals." In *Readings from Scientific American,* edited by Thomas Eisner and Edward O. Wilson. San Francisco: W. H. Freeman & Co., 1975, 279–82.

Ernst, Carl H. *Venomous Reptiles of North America.* Washington, D.C.: Smithsonian Institution Press, 1992.

Ferguson, Gary W. "Display and Communications in Reptiles: An Historical Perspective." *American Zoologist* 17:1 (winter 1977): 167–76.

Fitch, Henry S. "Ecological Studies of Lizards on the University of Kansas Natural History Reservation." In *Lizard Ecology: A Symposium,* edited by William W. Milstead. Columbia: University of Missouri Press, 1967, 30–44.

Frazer, J. G. *Totemism and Exogamy.* Vol. 4. London: Dawsons of Pall Mall, 1968. Orig. published 1910.

Fuhn, Ion E. "The Skinks." In *Grzimek's Animal Life Encyclopedia,* vol. 6, edited by Bernhard Grzimek. New York: Van Nostrand Reinhold, 1975, 242–63.

Gadow, Hans. *The Cambridge Natural History.* Vol. 8, *Amphibia and Reptiles.* Codicote, England: Wheldon & Wesley, Ltd., 1958. Orig. published 1901.

Gander, Frank F. "Fence Lizards in My Garden." In *The Audubon Book of True Nature Stories,* edited by John Terres. New York: Thomas Y. Crowell, 1958, 148–51.

Gans, Carl, and Donald W. Tinkle, eds. *Biology of the Reptilia.* Vol. 7, *Ecology and Behaviour.* London: Academic Press, 1977.

Gibbons, Whit. *Their Blood Runs Cold: Adventures with Reptiles and Amphibians.* Tuscaloosa: University of Alabama Press, 1983.

Gibbons, Whit, and Anne R. Gibbons. *Ecoviews: Snakes, Snails, and Environmental Tales.* Tuscaloosa: University of Alabama Press, 1998.

Gibbons, J. Whitfield, David Scott, Travis Ryan, Kurt Buhlmann, Tracey Tuberville, Brian Metts, Judith Greene, Tony Mills, Yale Leiden, Sean Poppy, and Christopher Winne. "The Global Decline of Reptiles, Déjà Vu Amphibians." *BioScience* 50:8 (August 2000): 653–66.

Goin, Olive B. *World Outside My Door.* New York: Macmillan, 1955.

Glasheen, James W., and Thomas A. McMahon. "Running on Water: The Secret of the Basilisk Lizard's Strategy Lies in Its Stroke." *Scientific American* 277:3 (September 1997): 68–9.

Greenberg, Bradley, and G. K. Noble. "Social Behavior of the American Chameleon (*Anolis carolinensis* Voigt)." *Physiological Zoology* 17:4 (1944): 392–439.

Greenberg, Neil. "A Neuroethological Study of Display Behavior in the Lizard *Anolis carolinensis* (Reptilia, Lacertilia, Iguanidae)." *American Zoologist* 17:1 (winter 1977): 191–201.

Greene, Harry W. *Snakes: The Evolution of Mystery in Nature.* Berkeley: University of California Press, 1997.

Grenard, Steve. *Medical Herpetology.* Pottsville, Penn.: N G Publishing Inc., 1994.

Gruber, Ulrich. "The Geckos and Their Relatives." In *Grzimek's Animal Life Encyclopedia,* vol. 6, edited by Bernhard Grzimek. New York: Van Nostrand Reinhold, 1975, 153–76.

Grzimek, Bernhard, ed. *Grzimek's Animal Life Encyclopedia.* Vol. 6, *Reptiles.* New York: Van Nostrand Reinhold, 1975.

Hansen, Robert, F. Wayne King, David Rodrigue, Andrew D. Walde, and John Wilkinson. *Discovery Channel Reptiles and Amphibians*. New York: Discovery Books, 2000.

Hartdegen, Ruston. "Herpetoculture of the Black Tree Monitor, *Veranus beccari.*" *Vivarium* 10:6 (October–November 1999): 20–2.

Hellmich, Walter. *Reptiles and Amphibians of Europe*. London: Blandford Press, 1962.

Henkel, Friedrich-Wilhelm, and Wolfgang Schmidt. *Geckoes: Biology, Husbandry, and Reproduction*. Trans. by John Hackworth. Malabar, FL: Krieger, 1995.

Hoser, Raymond T. *Australian Reptiles and Frogs*. Sydney, Australia: Pierson & Co., 1989.

Huey, Raymond B., Eric R. Pianka, and Thomas W. Schoener, eds. *Lizard Ecology: Studies of a Model Organism*. Cambridge, Mass: Harvard University Press, 1983.

Jackson, M. H. *Galápagos: A Natural History Guide*. Calgary, Alberta, Canada: University of Calgary Press, 1985.

Jenssen, Thomas A. "Evolution of Anoline Lizard Display Behavior." *American Zoologist* 17:1 (winter 1977): 203–15.

Kästle, Werner. "The Iguanids." In *Grzimek's Animal Life Encyclopedia*, vol. 6, edited by Bernhard Grzimek. New York: Van Nostrand Reinhold, 1975, 177–203.

Klemmer, Konrad. "The Lizards, An Introduction." In *Grzimek's Animal Life Encyclopedia*, vol. 6, edited by Bernhard Grzimek. New York: Van Nostrand Reinhold, 1975, 151–2.

———. "The True Lizards." In *Grzimek's Animal Life Encyclopedia*, vol. 6, edited by Bernhard Grzimek. New York: Van Nostrand Reinhold, 1975, 284–306.

Lamar, William W. *The World's Most Spectacular Reptiles and Amphibians*. Photos by Pete Carmichael and Gail Shumway. Tampa: World Publications, 1997.

Lane, Robert S., and G. B. Quist. "Borreliacidal Factor in the Blood of the Western Fence Lizard (*Sceloporus occidentalis*)." *Journal of Parasitology* 84:1 (February 1998): 29–34.

"Las Vegas Man Convicted of Smuggling Lizards in Underwear." CNN.com (Sept. 11, 2000).

"Legend of Lizard Man." *Time* 132:7 (August 15, 1988): 21.

Loveridge, Arthur. *Reptiles of the Pacific World*. New York: Macmillan, 1945.

Lubrano, Alfred. "Of Lizard People and Their Kept Reptiles." *Philadelphia Inquirer* (January 22, 2002).

Manaster, Jane. *Horned Lizards*. Austin: University of Texas Press, 1997.

Marcellini, Dale. "Acoustic and Visual Display Behavior of Gekkonid Lizards." *American Zoologist* 17:1 (winter 1977): 251–60.

Martin, James. *Masters of Disguise: A Natural History of Chameleons*. New York: Facts on File, 1992.

Masterman, Sue. "Antibiotic Dundee." ABCNews.com (May 26, 2000).

Mattison, Chris. *Lizards of the World*. London: Blandford, 1992.

McGinnity, Dale. "A Preliminary Assessment of the Conservation and Survival Status of West Indian Giant Galliwasps, with Recommendations for an Action Plan." Unpublished manuscript, February 2000.

Meloy, Ellen. *The Last Cheater's Waltz: Beauty and Violence in the Desert Southwest*. New York: Henry Holt, 1999.

Mercatante, Anthony. *Facts on File Encyclopedia of World Mythology and Legend*. New York: Facts on File, 1988: 642.

Mertens, Robert. *The World of Amphibians and Reptiles*. Trans. by H. W. Parker. New York: McGraw-Hill, 1960.

Milne, Lorus, and Margery Milne. "The Horned Toad—Desert Oddity." In *The Audubon Book of True Nature Stories*, edited by John Terres. New York: Thomas Y. Crowell, 1958, 172–5.

Milstead, William W., ed. *Lizard Ecology: A Symposium*. Columbia: University of Missouri Press, 1967.

Minton, Sherman A., Jr., and Madge Minton. *Venomous Reptiles*. New York: Scribner's, 1969.

———. *The Giant Reptiles*. New York: Scribner's, 1973.

Mitchell, Joseph C. *The Reptiles of Virginia*. Washington D. C.: Smithsonian Institution Press, 1994.

Moermond, Timothy C. "Habitat Constraints on the Behavior, Morphology, and Community Structure of *Anolis* Lizards." *Ecology* 60:1 (February 1979): 152–64.

Morris, Percy A. *An Introduction to the Reptiles and Amphibians of the United States*. New York: Dover, 1974. Orig. published 1944.

Neugebauer, Wilbert. "Monitors." In *Grzimek's Animal Life Encyclopedia*, vol. 6, edited by Bernhard Grzimek. New York: Van Nostrand Reinhold, 1975, 323–31.

Nogales, Manuel, Juan Rando, Alfredo Valido, and Aurelio Martin. "Discovery of a Living Giant Lizard, Genus *Gallotia* (Reptilia: Lacertidae), From La Gomera, Canary Islands." *Herpetologica* 57:2 (June 2001): 169–79.

Obst, Fritz J., Klaus Richter, and Udo Jacob. *The Completely Illustrated Atlas of Reptiles and Amphibians for the Terrarium*. Neptune City, N. J.: T.F.H. Publications, 1988.

Palmer, William M., and Alvin L. Braswell. *Reptiles of North Carolina*. Chapel Hill: University of North Carolina Press, 1995.

Petzold, H. G. "Lateral Fold Lizards." In *Grzimek's Animal Life Encyclopedia*, vol. 6, edited by Bernhard Grzimek. New York: Van Nostrand Reinhold, 1975, 307–16.

Pianka, Eric R. *The Lizard Man Speaks*. Austin: University of Texas Press, 1994.

Plotkin, Mark J. *Medicine Quest*. New York: Viking, 2000.

Pope, Clifford H. *The Reptile World*. New York: Knopf, 1956.

Pough, R. Harvey, Robin M. Andrews, John E. Cadle, Martha L. Crump, Alan H. Savitzky, and Kentwood D. Wells. *Herpetology*. Upper Saddle River, N. J.: Prentice Hall, 1998.

Preston-Mafham, Ken. *Madagascar: A Natural History*. Oxford: Facts on File, 1991.

Quammen, David. *Flight of the Iguana*. New York: Anchor Books, 1988.

———. *The Song of the Dodo*. New York: Scribner, 1996.

Reyes, Carl. "Jackson's Chameleon." Website: www.botany.hawaii.edu.

Richardson, Maurice. *The Fascination of Reptiles*. New York: Hill & Wang, 1972.

Rogner, Manfred. *Lizards*. Vol. 1: *Geckoes, Flap-Footed Lizards, Agamas, Chameleons, and Iguanas*. Trans. by John Hackworth. Malabar, FL: Krieger, 1997.

———. *Lizards*. Vol. 2: *Monitors, Skinks, and Other Lizards, Including Tuataras and Crocodilians*. Trans. by John Hackworth. Malabar, Fla.: Krieger, 1997.

Rothman, Robert. "Natural History of the Galápagos Islands." www.rit.edu/~rhrsbi/GalapagosPages/Galapagos.html.

Scherpner, Christoph. "Family: Teiidae." In *Grzimek's Animal Life Encyclopedia*, vol. 6, edited by Bernhard Grzimek. New York: Van Nostrand Reinhold, 1975, 275–83.

Schettino, L. R., ed. *The Iguanid Lizards of Cuba*. Gainesville: University Presses of Florida, 1999.

Schifter, Herbert. "Chameleons." In *Grzimek's Animal Life Encyclopedia*, vol. 6, edited by Bernhard Grzimek. New York: Van Nostrand Reinhold, 1975, 227–41.

Schmidt, Karl P., and Robert F. Inger. *Living Reptiles of the World*. Garden City, N.Y.: Hanover House, 1957.

Schwartz, Albert, and Robert W. Henderson. *Amphibians and Reptiles of the West Indies*. Gainesville: University Presses of Florida, 1991.

Shine, Richard. *Australian Snakes: A Natural History*. Ithaca, N.Y.: Cornell University Press, 1991.

Simon, Carol. "Masters of the Tongue Flick." *Natural History* 91:9 (September 1982): 58–67.

Simon, Hilda. *Chameleons and Other Quick-Change Artists*. New York: Dodd, Mead, 1973.

Smith, Hobart M. *Handbook of Lizards*. Ithaca, NY: Comstock/Cornell University Press, 1995. Orig. published 1946.

Sprackland, Robert G. *Giant Lizards*. Neptune City, NJ: T.F.H. Publications, 1992.

Staub, Rick. "A Namibian Adventure." *Reptiles Magazine* 8:7 (July 2000), 48–60.

Stebbins, Robert C. *Amphibians and Reptiles of Western North America*. New York: McGraw-Hill, 1954.

———. *A Field Guide to Western Reptiles and Amphibians*. 2d ed. Boston: Houghton Mifflin, 1985.

Stebbins, Robert C., and Richard M. Eakin. "The Role of the 'Third Eye' in Reptilian Behavior." *American Museum Novitates*, no. 1870 (February 26, 1958).

Taylor, Edward H. *Recollections of an Herpetologist*. Lawrence: University of Kansas Museum of Natural History, 1975.

Tinkham, Ernest B. "Biology of the Gila Monster." In *Venomous Animals and Their Venoms*, edited by Wolfgang Bücherl and Eleanor Buckley. New York: Academic Press, 1971.

Tobey, Franklin J., Jr. "The Mystery of Harvard's Civil War Lizard." *Civil War Times Illustrated* 24:6 (January-February 1991): 24–6.

Tyning, Thomas. *A Guide to Amphibians and Reptiles*. Boston: Little, Brown & Co., 1990.

Tyson, Peter. *The Eighth Continent: Life, Death, and Discovery in the Lost World of Madagascar*. New York: William Morrow, 2000.

Uetz, Peter. "How Many Reptile Species?" *Herpetological Review* 31:1 (March 2000): 13–14.

Vitt, Laurie J., Justin D. Congdon, and Nancy A. Dickson. "Adaptive Strategies and Energetics of Tail Autotomy in Lizards." *Ecology* 58:2 (early spring 1977): 326–37.

Vitt, Laurie J., and William E. Cooper Jr. "Tail Loss, Tail Color, and Predator Escape in *Eumeces* (Lacertilia: Scincidae): Age-Specific Differences in Costs and Benefits." *Canadian Journal of Zoology* 64:3 (March 1986): 583–92.

Von Geldern, Charles E. "Color Changes and Structure of the Skin of *Anolis carolinensis*." *Proceedings of the California Academy of Sciences* 10:10 (February 12, 1921): 77–117.

Watson, Lyall. *Jacobson's Organ and the Remarkable Nature of Smell*. New York: Norton, 2000.

Wermuth, Heinz. "Beaded Lizards." In *Grzimek's Animal Life Encyclopedia*, vol. 6, edited by Bernhard Grzimek. New York: Van Nostrand Reinhold, 1975, 321–3.

Wever, Ernest Glen. *The Reptile Ear: Its Structure and Function*. Princeton, N/ J.: Princeton University Press, 1978.

Wikelski, Martin, and Corinna Thom. "Marine Iguanas Shrink to Survive El Niño." *Nature* 403:6765 (January 6, 2000): 37–8.

Williams, Ernest E., and A. Stanley Rand. "Species Recognition, Dewlap Function and Faunal Size." *American Zoologist* 17:1 (winter 1977): 261–70.

Zimmer, Carl. "Get a Grip." *Natural History* 109:6 (July-August 2000): 42–3.

Male panther chameleon
Collectors and hobbyists find chameleons among the most fascinating of lizards. In captivity, however, many of these lizards suffer from stress, dehydration, improper nutrition, vitamin and mineral deficiencies, respiratory illnesses, and internal parasites—and consequently do not survive long.

Index

Aborigines, *21, 26*

Adams, Douglas, *144, 145*

Adler, Kraig, *148*

Agama (*Agama*), *26*

Agama, gliding (*Draco volans*), *19*

Agama, horned (*Agama lehmanni*), *31*

Allen, Woody, *21*

Ameiva, *53*

Amphibian population declines, *147*

Amphibians, *89, 148*

Angermeyer, Karl, *131*

Anguids (Family Anguidae), *47*

Anoles, *31, 36, 38, 42, 47, 50, 71, 74, 76*

Anole, Cuban brown (*Anolis sagrei*), *15*

Anole, green (*Anolis carolinensis*), *98–99, 147*

Anole, Jamaican giant or crown super-giant (*Anolis garmani*), *31, 52, 100–101*

Anole, Smallwood's giant (*Anolis smallwoodi*), *31*

Aphrodisiac, *26*

Aporosaura anchietae, *84*

Auffenberg, Walter, *32, 144*

Austin Lounge Lizards, *21*

Autotomy, *61–63, 81*

Barbour, Roger, *125*

Barker, Will, *42, 123*

Bartlett, R. D., *96, 100, 109*

Bartlett, Patricia P., *96, 100, 109*

Basilisks (*Basiliscus*), *42*

Beccari, Odouardo, *137*

Bauer, Aaron, *55, 65*

Beach Lizards, *21*

Beebe, William, *130*

Behavior, *71–87*

Bellairs, Angus, *55, 71, 86*

Big Nick and the Gila Monsters, *21*

Blair, W. Frank, *47, 57, 74, 86, 116, 118*

Bogert, Charles, *47, 57, 74, 86, 116, 118*

Brattstrom, Bayard, *71*

Breckenridge, W. J., *123*

Brown, David, *116, 118*

Budweiser chameleons, *21, 15*

Burghardt, Gordon, *130*

Burton, Maurice, *74, 124*

Burton, Robert, *74, 124*

Canary Islands, *74, 148*

Capote, Truman, *89, 98*

Caribbean Anole Database, *100*

Carmony, Neil, *116, 118*

Carr, Archie, *26, 63, 71, 78, 98, 112, 119, 147*

Carrington, Richard, *71*

Carwardine, Mark, *144, 145*

Cejudo, Daniel, *78*

Chace, G. Earl, *118*

Chameleons, *21, 24, 26, 31, 36, 38, 42, 47–48, 52, 55, 57, 61, 71, 72, 75, 84*

Chamaeleo chamaeleon, *95*

Chameleon, crested (*Chamaeleo cristatus*), *32*

Chameleon, Cuban false (*Chamaeleolis chamaeleonides*), *50*

Chameleon, flap-necked (*Chamaeleo dilepis*), *60, 95*

Chameleon, Jackson's (*Chamaeleo jacksonii*), *31, 36, 48, 89, 90–91*

Chameleon, Johnston's (*Chamaeleo johnstoni johnstoni*), *31*

Chameleon, mountain (*Chamaeleo [Trioceros] montium*), *31, 96–97*

Chameleon, panther (*Furcifer pardalis*), *7, 38, 49, 71, 92–93, 156*

Chameleon, Parson's (*Chamaeleo pasoni*), *14*

Chameleon, sail-finned (*Chamaeleo cristatus*), *36*

Chameleon, Senegal (*Chamaeleo senegalensis*), *17, 46*

Chameleon, veiled (*Chamaeleo calyptratus*), *19, 73*

Charles Darwin Research Station, *132, 151*

Cherry, Jim, *19, 21*

Chuckwalla (*Sauromalus obesus*), *26, 36, 71, 78*

Ciofi, Claudio, *144*

Circulatory system, *65–66*

Climate change, *147, 148*

Convention on International Trade in Endangered Species of Wild Fauna and Flora (CITES), *148*

Cloaca, *66, 71, 76*

Collins, Joseph T., *118*

Colnett, James, *130*

Coloration, *36–40, 63, 71, 74, 75, 76, 78, 83, see also individual species*

Communication, *36, 52, 53, 74–76, 78*

Conant, Roger, *118*

Conservation, *147–152*

Cooper Jr., William E., *63*

Courtship behavior, *31, 36, 71, 74, 75*

Crests, *31, 32, 36, 71*

Crocodilians, *89*

Dallas Zoo, *137*

Darwin, Charles, *26, 29, 130, 132, 152*

Defense strategies, *36, 38, 57, 61, 78–83*

de la Cepede, Count, *26, 47, 57*

de Vosjoli, Philippe, *105*

del Campo, Rafael Martin, *57, 86, 116, 118*

Dewlap, *31, 36, 47, 71, 74, 76*

Digestive system, *66*

Dinosaurs, *19*

Diseases, *147, 148*

Distel, Hansjurgen, *130*

Distribution, *89–90, see also individual species*

Ditmars, Raymond L., *36, 57, 61, 112, 116, 119, 120, 123, 134*

Draco, *19*

Dragons, *19*

Dragon, bearded (*Pogona*), *36, 78*

Dragon, flying (*Draco volans*), *36, 42, 71*

Dragon, Komodo (*Varanus komodoensis*), *32, 52, 78, 81, 84, 140, 141, 142–145, 151*

Dragon, sailfin (*Hydrosaurus amboinensis*), *66*

Ears, *52–53*

Ectothermy, *68, 86*

Egg tooth, *57, 72*

Eggs, *63, 71–72*

Eibl-Eibesfeldt, Irenaus, *127*

Estivation, *61, 63, 86*

Etzold, T., *89*

European Molecular Biology Laboratory, *89*

Excretory system, *66*

Eyes, *36, 47–50*

Families and species, *89–145*

Fancy Lizards, *21*

Fast, Frank, *105*

Femoral glands, *76*

Fitch, Henry S., *112, 124*

Folklore, *see Myths*

Frazer, J. G., *21*

Freshman, The, *19*

Frogs, *36, 47, 74*

Gadow, Hans, *129, 132*

Galápagos Islands, *20, 29, 68, 69, 84, 127, 130, 132, 133, 151, 152*

Galápagos National Park Service, *132*

Galliota gomerana, *148*

Galliwasps (*Diploglossus*), *151*

Gander, Frank, *125*

Gecko, banded (*Coleonyx variegatus*), *151*

Gecko, barking (*Underwoodisaurus milii*), *74*

Gecko, blue-tailed day, (*Phelsuma cepediana*), *25, 40*

Gecko, Central American banded (*Coleonyx mitratus*), *151*

Gecko, crested or eyelash (*Rhacodactylus ciliatus*), *7, 44, 47, 48, 104–105*

Gecko, *Diplodactylus*, *61*

Gecko, day (*Phelsuma*), *74*

Gecko, dwarf (*Sphaerodactylus ariasae*), *32*

Gecko, fat-tailed (*Hemitheconyx caudicinctus*), *37, 63, 108–109*

Gecko, flat-tailed (*Uroplatus fimbriatus*), *74*

Gecko, frog-eyed, (*Teratoscincus cincus roborowskii*), 49

Gecko, golden (*Gekko auratus* or *Gekko ulikovskii*), 54

Gecko, leaf-tailed (*Uroplatus*), 42, 49, 78

Gecko, lined leaf-tailed, (*Uroplatus lineatus*), 38, 44

Gecko, leopard (*Eublepharis macularius*), 52, 106–107, 149

Gecko, Madagascan giant day (*Phelsuma madagascariensis grandis*), 7, 71, 102–103

Gecko, marbled (*Gekko monarchus*), 23

Gecko, Namib Desert (*Palmatogecko rangei*), 7, 11

Gecko, parachute (*Ptychozoon kuhli*), 42

Gecko, tokay (*Gekko gecko*), 24, 72, 74

Gehyra mutilata, 36

Giant Gila Monster, The, 19

Gibbons, Whit, 26, 147

Gila monster (*Heloderma suspectum*), 24, 36, 57, 59, 61, 65, 78, 86, 116–118, 151

Glasheen, James W., 42

Goannas (*Varanus*), 26, 137

Godzilla, 15, 19

Goin, Olive, 118

Gould, John, 137

Greenberg, Bradley, 71

Greene, Harry, 65, 130

Grinning Lizards, 21

Gruber, Ulrich, 74

Habitat destruction, 147, 148

Hale, Bruce, 21

Hartdegen, Ruston, 137

Harvard Museum, 124

Hau, David, 142

Head bobbing, 38, 71, 74

Heads, 31, 32

Hearing, 36, 52–53

Heart, 65

Hemipenis, 66, 71

Henkel, Friedrich-Wilhelm, 36, 71, 74, 81, 102, 105

Herpetological Conservation Trust, 148

Hetherington, Thomas, 52

Hibernation, 48, 61, 63, 86–87

Hollywood films, 19, 21, 128, 130

Honolulu Zoo, 140

Hopi Indians, 120

Horned Lizard Conservation Society, 120, 148

Horns, 31, 71, 78, 89, 90, 96–97

Horny Toads, 21

Hoser, Raymond, 137

Humans and lizards, 10–29, 84, 147–148

Iguana, black (*Ctenosaura similis*), 57

Iguana, Galápagos land (*Conolophus subcristatus, Conolophus pallidus*), 26, 29, 84, 132–133

Iguana, green (*Iguana iguana*), 26, 128–130

Iguana, Jamaican (*Cyclura collei*), 151

Iguana, marine (*Amblyrhynchus cristatus*), 68, 69, 84, 130–131, 152

Iguana, rhinoceros (*Cyclura cornuta*), 31, 134–135

Iguana, rock (*Cyclura nubila lewisi*), 135

Inger, Robert, 26, 42, 47, 50, 74, 78, 98, 118, 119, 124, 130

Internal anatomy, 64–66

International Union for the Conservation of Nature, 148

Invasive species, 147, 148

Jackson, M. H., 127, 130, 132

Jacobson, Ludwig, 55

Jacobson's organ, 54, 55, 76

Johnston, Tony, 21

Jurassic Park, 78, 90

Kästle, Werner, 130

Kentropyx calcaratus, 72

Komodo, 19

Komodo Island, 143, 144

Komodo National Park, 151

Lacerta, 87

Lamellae, 42

Lane, Robert, 151

Leapin' Lizards, 21

Lewis, Meriwether, 120

Limbs, 42, 64, 65

Linneaus, Carolus, 19

Lizard, African plated (*Gerrhosaurus*), 72

Lizard, Mexican beaded (*Heloderma horridum*), 57, 61, 65, 78, 116

Lizard, blind (*Dibamus, Anelytropsis*), 47

Lizard, caiman (*Dracaena*), 84

Lizard, California legless (*Anniella pulchra*), 47

Lizard, collared (*Crotaphytus collaris*), 42, 78

Lizard, crevice spiny (*Sceloporus poinsetti*), 78

Lizard, Eastern collared (*Crotaphytus c. collaris*), 122–123

Lizard, Eastern glass (*Ophisaurus ventralis*), 13, 118–119

Lizard, fence or Eastern fence, (*Sceloporus undulatus*), 71, 83

Lizard, Fernand's (*Riopa fernandi*), *see* Skink, fire

Lizard, frilled (*Chlamydosaurus kingii*), 31, 36, 74, 78

Lizard, girdle-tailed (*Cordylus*), 78

Lizard, granite spiny, (*Sceloporus orcutti*), 126

Lizard, horned (*Phrynosoma*), 31, 36, 78, 84

Lizard, Jesus Christ (*Basiliscus basiliscus*), 42

Lizard, lava, (*Tropidurus*), 127

Lizard, leopard (*Gambelia wislizenii*), 43

Lizard, rock (*Lacerta*), 47

Lizard, rusty or Texas spiny (*Sceloporus olivaceous*), 47

Lizard, sand-diving (*Aporasaura*), 68

Lizard, short-horned (*Phrynosoma douglasii*), 72, 81, 120–121

Lizard, Sierra fence (*Sceloporus occidentalis taylori*), 15

Lizard, spiny-tailed (*Uromastix*), 26, 36

Lizard, tiger (*Nucras*), 78

Lizard, Western collared (*Crotaphytus c. baileyi*), 123

Lizard, Western fence (*Sceloporus occidentalis*), 124, 151

Lizard, whiptail (*Cnemidophorus*), 55, 72

Lizard, zebra-tailed (*Callisaurus draconoides*), 42

Lizard Lick, North Carolina, 24

Lizard Man, 24, 26

Lizard Mound County Park, 24

Lizard Train, 21

LizArt, 15

Loco for Lizards, 19

Locomotion, 42–44

London Zoo, 144

Los Angeles Zoo, 144

Loveridge, Arthur, 144

Lyme disease, 151

Madagascar, 40

Manaster, Jane, 78, 120

Marcellini, Dale, 144

Marquez, Rafael, 78

Martin, James, 24, 31, 36, 71, 72, 92, 93, 95

Mastigures (*Uromastyx*), 68

Mattison, Chris, 36, 38, 47, 71, 72, 78, 84, 111

McGinnity, Dale, 134, 151

McMahon, T. A., 42

Meade, Gen. George, 124

Medicinal uses for lizards, 26, 118, 148, 151

Megalania prisca, 32

Meloy, Ellen, 68

Mercatante, Anthony, 21

Mertens, Robert, 38, 42, 86, 96

Miller, Brian, 123, 151

Milne, Lorus, 72

Milne, Margery, 72

Minton, Madge, 24

Minton, Sherman, 24

Mitchell, Joseph, 119, 124

Monitor, black tree (*Varanus beccarii*), *137*

Monitor, black-headed (*Varanus tristis*), *21*

Monitor, Bornean earless (*Varanus borneensis*), *52*

Monitor, crocodile (*Varanus salvadorii*), *38, 140–141*

Monitor, Gould's (*Varanus flavirufus*), *137–140*

Monitor, green tree (*Varanus prasinus*), *137*

Monitor, Indian (*Varanus indicus*), *26*

Monitor, Nile (*Varanus niloticus*), *26*

Monitor, savannah (*Varanus exanthematicus*), *78*

Monitor, water (*Varanus salvator*), *26, 140*

Morris, Percy, *124*

Morrison, Jim, *21*

Munich Lounge Lizards, *21*

Myths, *13, 19, 21, 24, 26*

Nashville Zoo, *151*

National Zoo, *145*

Native Americans, *24, 26*

Naultinus elegans, 71–72

New York Zoological Park, *134*

Nictitating membrane, *47*

Noble, G. K., *71*

On Moonshine Mountain, 19

One Million B.C., 19

Ornamentation, *see* Crests; Horns

Oviparity, *71*

Ovoviviparity, *71*

Parasites, *147, 148*

Parietal eye, *48*

Parthenogenesis, *72*

Partners in Amphibian and Reptile Conservation, *148*

Perentie (*Varanus giganteus*), *21*

Pet trade, *15, 26, 105, 148*

Pheromones, *112*

Physical characteristics, *31–68*

Physical posturing, *74, see also* Head bobbing; Push-ups

Pianka, Eric, *11, 26, 61, 63, 78, 81, 84, 98*

Pinkwater, Daniel, *21*

Plated lizard, Eritrean, *(Gerrhosaurus validus), 55, 72*

Pliny, *26*

Plotkin, Mark J., *151*

Pollution, *147, 148, 152*

Pop, Iggy, *21*

Pope, Clifford H., *15, 19, 21, 31, 42, 44, 47, 76, 84, 114, 120, 123, 124*

Pough, F. Harvey, *48, 65, 68, 72, 89, 98*

Predation, *84*

Preston-Mafham, Ken, *55, 102*

Proctoporus shrevei, 76

Pseudocopulation, *72*

Push-ups, *71, 74*

Quammen, David, *32, 36, 130, 131, 142*

Racerunner, prairie (*Cnemidophorus sexlineatus viridis*), *123*

Racerunner, six-lined (*Cnemidophorus sexlineatus*), *42, 123–124*

Rand, A. Stanley, *130*

Reproduction, *66, 71–73*

Reptilia, *89*

Reptile population declines, *147*

Reptile Rearing Center, *132*

Reyes, Carl, *90*

Richardson, Maurice, *74, 129*

Rogner, Manfred, *96, 109, 111, 114, 123, 130*

Roosevelt, Theodore, *26*

Rothman, Robert, *132*

Royal Society for Prevention of Cruelty to Animals, *26*

Russell, Findlay, *57*

Salamanders, *36*

Salmonella, *26*

Salvadori, Tommaso, *140*

San Diego Zoo, *15*

Scales, *32, 36, 38, 78, 83*

Scherpner, Christoph, *123*

Schifter, Herbert, *95*

Schmidt, Karl, *26, 42, 47, 50, 74, 78, 98, 118, 119, 124, 130*

Schmidt, Wolfgang, *36, 71, 74, 81, 102*

Shakespeare, William, *21*

Shape, *31, see also individual species*

Sharmat, Marjorie W., *21*

Shine, Richard, *86*

Simon, Hilda, *38*

Size, *32, see also individual species*

Skin, *26, 36–38*

shedding of, *36, 37, 72, 81*

Skink, blue-tailed (*Eumeces*), *26*

Skink, blue-tongued (*Tiliqua*), *26, 78*

Skink, fire, *(Riopa fernandi), 24, 27*

Skink, five-lined (*Eumeces fasciatus*), *57, 62, 63, 76, 84, 86, 112–113*

Skink, prairie (*Eumeces septentrionalis*), *86*

Skink, prehensile-tailed or giant (*Corucia zebrata*), *11, 61, 83, 114*

Skink, sand (*Scincus scincus*), *69*

Skinks, *Prasinohaema, 66*

Slow worm (*Anguis fragilis*), *31, 151*

Smell, sense of, *55–57*

Smith, Hobart, *36, 42, 61, 65, 68, 74, 89, 118, 120, 123, 126*

Snakes, *26, 36, 37, 47, 55, 57, 6566, 71, 78, 89*

Snake, brown tree, *148*

Society for the Study of Amphibians and Reptiles, *148*

Spielberg, Steven, *78, 90*

Sprackland, Robert, *19, 32, 72, 137, 140, 144*

Staub, Rick, *111*

Stebbins, Robert, *47, 52, 57, 68, 78, 116, 124, 126*

Superstitions, *57, 93*

Swift (*Sceloporus*), *78*

Swift, emerald (*Sceloporus malachiticus*), *64*

Swing Lizards, *21*

Tails, *31, 42, 46, 60–63, 66, 73, 74, 76, 78, 81*

Taste, sense of, *55–57*

Taylor, Edward H., *71*

Teeth, *57–59, 65*

Tegus (*Tupinambis*), *42*

Thermoregulation, *48, 68–69*

Thom, Corinna, *131*

Thorny devil (*Moloch horridus*), *68, 84*

Thundering Lizards, *21*

Tobey Jr., Franklin, *124*

Toe pads, *42*

Tortoise, Galápagos, *132*

Tuatara, *89*

Türk, Hanne, *21*

Tyning, Thomas, *52, 112*

Uetz, Peter, *89*

Unsustainable harvesting, *147, 148*

U.S. Endangered Species Act, *148*

Urinary system, *66*

van der Waals force, *42*

Varanus gouldii, see Monitor, Gould's (*Varanus flavirufus*)

Veazey, J., *130*

Venom, *36, 47–50*

Vision, *36, 47–50*

Vitt, Laurie, *63*

Viviparity, *71*

Wall Street, 21

Water dragon, Asian green (*Physignathus concincinus*), *31, 35*

Watson, Lyall, *55*

Wever, Ernest, *52*

Wikelski, Martin, *131*

World Conservation Union, *151*

Woods, Charles, *24*

Yosemite National Park, *15*

Zelig, 21

Zulus, *21*

Zurich Zoo, *26*

About the Author
and Photographer

David Badger lives in Franklin, Tennessee, with his wife, Sherry, and son, Jeff. He is professor of journalism and assistant director of the School of Journalism at Middle Tennessee State University, where he teaches magazine writing, feature writing, media writing, arts reviewing, and motion picture history. He reviewed films for WPLN-FM public radio in Nashville for thirteen years, and wrote book reviews and columns for the Nashville *Tennessean* for seventeen years. He grew up in Wilmette, Illinois, and earned an A.B. degree in English literature from Duke University, M.S.J. degree in editorial journalism from Northwestern University, and Ph.D. in communication from the University of Tennessee.

He is the author of *Frogs* (Voyageur Press, 1995), *Snakes* (Voyageur Press, 1999), and *Frogs: WorldLife Library* (Voyageur Press, 2000), all illustrated with photographs by John Netherton. He is the coauthor of *Newscraft*, a contributor to *Free Expression and the American Public*, and the editor of nine books by John Netherton.

The late John Netherton, a nature photographer for more than thirty years, was a resident of Nashville, Tennessee, and the father of three sons, Jason, Josh, and Erich. His photographs have appeared in numerous magazines, including *Audubon*, *Natural History*, *National Wildlife*, *Nikon World*, *Outside*, *Popular Photography*, *Birder's World*, and *WildBird*, and he wrote a regular column for *Outdoor Photographer*. At the time of his death in March 2001 he was president of Friends of Radnor Lake, in Nashville, and a member of the Nature's Best Foundation Advisory Board. *American Photographer* named him a Friend of the Earth, and he was presented the Governor's Outstanding Tennessean Award in 1998.

John Netherton (left) and David Badger.
Photograph © Rob Hoffman

His work has been featured in more than twenty of his own books, including *Radnor Lake: Nature's Walden*; *A Guide to Photography and the Smoky Mountains*; *Florida: A Guide to Nature and Photography*; *Tennessee: A Homecoming*; *Big South Fork Country* (with Senator Howard Baker); *At the Water's Edge: Wading Birds of North America* (Voyageur Press, 1994); *Tennessee Wonders: A Pictorial Guide to the Parks*; *Tennessee: A Bicentennial Celebration*; *Scott's Gulf: The Bridgestone/Firestone Centennial Wilderness* (with Senator Howard Baker); and *Frogs* (Voyageur Press, 1995), *Snakes* (Voyageur Press, 1999), and *Frogs: WorldLife Library* (Voyageur Press, 2000), all with David Badger.